God's Restorative Nature

NANCY HULSHULT
CHAD P. SHEPHERD

God's Restorative Nature

ISBN: 979-8-9856988-1-7

Published by:
NarratusCreative | Narratus Press
P.O. Box 1413
Hamilton, OH 45012

Design: NarratusCreative | narratuscreative.com
Cover Photo Credits: Denise Chaney, Evan Hulshult, Nancy Hulshult and Sterling Shepherd.

Produced in the United States of America

DEDICATION

This book is dedicated to our parents, grandparents, and great grandparents, who have given us a legacy of spirituality and love for God.

THANKS & APPRECIATION

Thanks to Mary Lou Hudek, Debbie Day, Nancy Teepen, and all who have helped us to edit, rethink, rewrite, and finalize our stories to share with others.

Thanks to those who are included in these stories, as you have inspired us to see the world in a better light for better days.

Thanks to our mentor and guide, Pastor Tim Kufeldt, who serves as our role model through his spiritual leadership and passion for missions.

Thanks to our contributing writers, Mark Banks, Dr. Chance Bosch, Nancy Teepen, Pastor Tyler Green, our children and grandchildren. The inclusion of your stories has greatly enhanced our theme of God at work in our lives.

Table of Contents

FOREWORD

Throughout these pages you will discover vignettes that will encourage, challenge, and inspire you to discover God at work in unexpected places. Chad and Nancy uncover their own personal journeys that reveal a tapestry of God at work in their lives. Whether in success or in failure, we can see the Divine handiwork weaving lives, nature, and opportunities together to reveal God's grace and love. On the underside we might find questions, confusion, and chaos. But when the work is done, we can see the stitching of color, of friends, of family, of success and failure coming together to form a beautiful artwork.

In these stories we can relate to the brutal honesty of failure and to the gentle confirmation of restoration as Chad reflects on his own story. We can see the serendipitous work of divine appointments and the merging of life experiences as Nancy reveals how God gives us light for our next footstep, even though we might be hoping for a floodlight for our future.

As I read these stories, there are moments when I found myself laughing out loud and other times when I brushed away a tear. Nancy, Chad, and friends invite us into their lives as they share moments of their lives. I invite you to receive their reflections. Perhaps God will speak to your heart of how He often chooses the ordinary to accomplish the extraordinary.

But we have this treasure in jars of clay, to show that the surpassing power belongs to God and not to us.

2 Corinthians 4:7 (ESV)

Pastor Tim Kufeldt
Dayspring Church
Forest Park, Cincinnati, Ohio

FOREWORD

Restoration: An act of restoring, or the condition of being restored.

> Joel 2:25-26 (ESV): *I will restore to you the years that the swarming locust has eaten, the cankerworm, and the caterpillar, and the palmerworm, my great army which I have sent among you.*
> *And, ye shall eat in plenty, and be satisfied, and Praise the name of the Lord your God, that hath dealt wondrously with you: and my people shall never be ashamed.*

How each of us yearn for an unblemished restoration!

As you read through these personal autobiographical experiences, you should easily be able to find a connection with your own personal journey. We have each dealt with life's challenges where, if we admit it, or not, our tribulations have evolved us. Whether it results in a callus, a scar, or we are left with an open wound, our desire and hope is for an absolute restoration.

In many of these life experiences, there is no complete absolution, no delusion of perfection, or fictional storybook finale. Each contains a declaration of growth, adjustment, and personal resolution.

As I read through these revealing journalistic chapters, I was often reconnected to my own personal timeline, as Chad is my nephew. Our own life span has been interwoven not only through the connection of family, but also the benefit of being a trusted and loyal friend.

While I remember him as a newborn baby, the Preble County student from the story, the father of three, the Guatemalan school principal, and now the co-author of this book, I am reminded how hearing these narrative accounts brings back so many other memories.

Chad and I have covered a lot of ground. We have produced many ideas and conceived many adventurous plans either by phone, or by international email. Where one is pensive, the other is unnerved, which could explain how we ended up in a 13 passenger van with two dogs and two turtles while driving from Guatemala to Ohio. I am sure this will be a topic in his next book.

Studying each drafted word has allowed me to reexamine the trials and tribulations of each of these life experiences. We have lived a lifetime, and with that we have lived through many life changing events. What I see is not the imperfection, but an evolution of complete restoration and the fulfillment of God's promise of redemption.

May this book help others, as it has helped me.

Stephen J. Mathis

God's Restorative Nature

Introduction—Nancy Hulshult

God is a perfect being, and we are imperfect human beings. We will never be perfect as God is perfect, and God cannot exist where there is not pureness, wholeness, and perfection. How and where can the perfect and imperfect exist together? How do we connect? How do we communicate with God unless our communicative space is purified somehow?

Adam and Eve in Nature

In the beginning, humans were formed in nature and placed in a perfect, purest place of nature, the Garden of Eden. God's original design was to walk and talk with humans with no barriers, until they sinned against him. Genesis 3:8 describes God as "walking in the garden in the cool of the day" when Adam and Eve hid from the Lord from fear and shame because they had disobeyed him. After that, God banished them from the Garden into the world to work the ground for their food. After that, many times God either sent messengers in human form (known as angels) or He used the forces of nature as a bridge to be able to communicate with his now imperfect beings.

Moses and God Alone in Nature

Moses heard from God through a burning bush. Not only did God get Moses' attention through a bush that was not totally consumed by the fire, but the space between them was purified through the fire. In this way, God and man could easily share the time and space for Moses to receive his special calling and purpose from God.

There the angel of the Lord appeared to him in flames of fire from within a bush. Moses saw that though the bush was on fire it did not burn up. So Moses thought, "I will go over and see this strange sight—why the bush does not burn up." When the Lord saw that he had gone over to look, God called to him from within the bush, "Moses! Moses!"

And Moses said, "Here I am."

"Do not come any closer," God said. "Take off your sandals, for the place where you are standing is holy ground." Then he said, "I am the God of your father,[a] the God of Abraham, the God of Isaac and the God of Jacob." At this, Moses hid his face, because he was afraid to look at God.
—Exodus 3:2-22-30 (NIV)

Through God's unusual use of nature, Moses was able to receive the message that he would be the leader to save the Israelites from the bondage of slavery in Egypt. God guided the Israelites out of Egypt through the visible sign of a cloud, and in Deuteronomy 21:15 the Lord appeared to Moses at the tent in a pillar of cloud.

Jacob and God alone in Nature

Another example of God meeting man in nature is the story of Jacob wrestling with an angel all night. Jacob had stolen Esau's birthright and was now attempting to reconcile with his brother by meeting him and giving him gifts. Jacob was ridden with fear, and in Genesis 32:11, he says to God, "Save me, I pray, from the hand of my brother Esau, for I am afraid he will come and attack me, and also the mothers with their children."

God waited to answer after Jacob was left completely alone in his camp. Jacob had sent his two wives and eleven sons to the other side of the ford of the Jabbok when an angel from God appeared to Jacob, and the two wrestled all night, leaving Jacob with a wrenched hip. By surviving this struggle and encountering

God face to face, the Lord renamed Jacob and called him Israel: a sign of a significant life change and calling from God.

> Then the man said, "Your name will no longer be Jacob, but Israel,[f] because you have struggled with God and with humans and have overcome." —Genesis 32:28 NIV
>
> So Jacob called the place Peniel, saying, "It is because I saw God face to face, and yet my life was spared." —Genesis 32:30 NIV

Jesus and God in Nature in Baptism

In the New Testament, God communicates through the sign of a dove when Jesus is baptized by John in the river.

As soon as Jesus was baptized, he went up out of the water. At that moment heaven was opened, and he saw the Spirit of God descending like a dove and alighting on him. (Matthew 3:16 NIV)

While there are stories in the Bible of people seeing God face to face and hearing from God through his voice and through messengers, we see many examples of God working through nature to communicate with his people. When we want to seek God, to communicate with him in a personal way, we can do this by opening our minds and spirits through various avenues: prayer, worship, reading God's Word in the Bible, hearing God's Word through messengers or prophets. We can also find God in his creation, in nature, in spaces that cause us to communicate with Him in unusual ways.

This book was written as an exploration into the many ways that we can be impacted by nature to communicate with God. Chad and I, as well as the contributing authors, have dedicated our lives to serving God through our work in missions, churches, schools, careers, and family life. We don't claim to be perfect beings, but our intentions are to please our perfect Creator.

When we met on the mission field in Guatemala, Chad and I

served in different roles: Chad as the missionary serving as liaison between the native people and the North American work campers, and I as the leader for children's ministries. Seven years later, we reconnected through social media to realize that our lives had changed dramatically since Guatemala and that we both love to write. Through a few exchanges, we decided to weave our stories together to see what God would do through our combined efforts. We challenged each other to be more reflective and to ensure that God gets the glory in our testimonies of his restorative power through nature. We agreed that we have a responsibility to tell our stories about God's creative and restorative power through his Holy Spirit, through people, and through nature.

Also contributing stories are Dr. Chance Bosch, Pastor Tyler Green, Nancy Teepen, Mark Banks, Chad's daughter Aleksandra Shepherd, and my oldest grandchildren. Chancey and I worked together in an alternative school setting many years ago. We focused on educating and healing the whole child through creative teaching methods and special events designed to help the students feel valued.

Pastor Tyler Green and his leadership team supported the freshmen students in my school where I was principal. They responded to my requests for extra grief support in times of school-wide crisis, motivational speeches at awards assemblies, quarterly rewards for academics and character, supervision of student-led before-school prayer groups, and evening all-city youth revivals held at our school.

Nancy Weisbrodt Teepen is a lifelong friend who has served as a teacher and church leader over the years. We helped each other while raising our young kids, working in church programs, and teaching in the same schools early in our education careers. We have frequent conversations about spirituality and the nature of God.

Mark Banks is a neighbor and lifelong storyteller about the

Native American traditions. He and his family present programs in schools and public events to educate and to remind people of the importance of the Native American culture to our rich history. His overriding message is one of inclusion and valuing all individuals, regardless of culture, creed, or age.

Humans share a common bond with nature. All are created by God. As the top tier in God's order of creation, we humans can inspire and be inspired. We know that God uses everything for his purpose. To this end, we hope we may inspire others to see God at work in their lives through nature, in nature, and with nature. Be blessed, and enjoy.

1

CHADDY BOY, THE PREACHER BOY

CHAD P. SHEPHERD

I heard the gravel crunch under my tires as I pulled over next to my old elementary school. With the windows down, the wind carried with it the memories of the sounds of the playground and the smell of crayons, paste, and erasers in a cardboard school box. I was immersed in the memories. A block away I could see the abandoned old mill, and George's Market. I used to go in there and get Kahn's bologna with my dad. I swore I'd never return to this place.

Just up the road I'd been knocked off my bike by three punks my age. I was a coward, but they tried to steal my new bike. Somehow I fought them off, all three of them, and peddled away with my heart pounding, my lungs screaming for air. That must have been about 33 years ago. I was short throughout school and a year younger than my classmates. I was chubby with buck teeth and glasses. I was an only child and didn't really like other kids. By the time I'd graduated, I learned how to use my fists to back off the bullies. Funny thing, the boys I fought would always end up being my friends. Even then adversity somehow would work its way out. That has kind of always been a theme with me.

My three best friends, though, I never fought. Well, I guess that isn't true. Kevin Dyehouse once tickled me to the point that I climbed a tree to try to get away from him. Then my mom showed up and told me I needed to punch him. I dropped from the tree and punched him in the gut. I still remember what he said when my ten year old fist hit its mark, "Chaddy boy, you hit me!"

In fifth grade we had a career day. We were supposed to dress up as our ideal career. I had no idea what to do. My greatest ambition at the time was to ride the back of the garbage truck. That job seemed fun. Instead, I put on pants, a white shirt, and a tie. I carried my Bible and told them I was going to grow up and be a preacher. That was the day I got my new nickname. Chaddy-boy became Preacher Boy. That name stuck and I hated it.

Kevin, Jerry, sometimes Larry, and sometimes April, and I would run the hills and creeks. We'd play flashlight tag and organize hedge apple fights. There was a wild man named Clint who was a few years older than we were, and he'd terrorize us all. Oh, the stories I could tell.

In elementary school, Kevin and I, our friend Kelly Staton, and Ken Menke convinced the entire third grade that "The Bloody Hand" was crawling around the cemetery next door. The principal intervened after we had every student standing at the far end of the playground, all straining to see the Bloody Hand that the three of us claimed to see. It got so deep we'd convinced ourselves that it was real... and none of us would dare admit otherwise.

I looked at the dashboard of my car and realized that it was nearly ten o'clock. I moved the stick into drive, checked my side mirror, and pulled back onto old State Route 503. My mind went to government class, my senior year. I can still hear the voice of that teacher, "I guarantee you that you all say you hate high school, but I can promise you, within five years, all of you will make a visit back here. You'll walk these halls and wish you could come back."

I laughed to myself. No way. I'll never come back to these hallways. I'll never sit alone again at lunch. I'll never see your faces. I'm getting out of this place. That was in 1992, and I've not been back since that rainy graduation day in June. It's nearly been 30 years, and I've not even driven past that high school building since then.

And yet, I no longer am opposed to the idea. I held the school record for tardies, and I had sneaked out early every day of my senior year. I'd leave early to go work for Gough Lamb Dry Cleaners for $4.25 an hour. I crashed their truck three times. They didn't seem to care, except for the time the owner was in the truck.

Now I race down State Route 503 with the windows down in the darkness. I am here, Preble County. Chaddy-boy, the Preacher boy, has been around the world, found success, made mistakes, lost everything more than once, and got it all back nearly every time. I am who I am, and this time there are no bullies that intimidate me. I've seen enough to fear confrontation no longer. I've won enough to know who I am, and I've lost enough to realize that I'm not strong enough to live life alone.

Life is a story, and if you're reading this now, there's a good chance that we're living in the same pages. Everyone has a story. We simply decide whether or not we'll tell it, and how we live will determine whether or not anyone will care to listen.

I've been around the world. I married the girl that I took to prom my senior year. We had a son and then adopted two daughters from Russia and China. We had a big house and shiny cars. We gave it all away and moved to Guatemala. We attempted to found an orphanage and lost everything. We planted a church of English speaking missionaries and Spanish speaking Guatemalans that grew to nearly 500 members. We did relief projects in third world villages and built hundreds of homes. We saw amazing stories and unexplainable miracles. Then we came back to the U.S. exhausted. We fell apart. After 24 years of marriage, we divorced. We just split up our assets and bills, considerable from Guatemala, and we walked away.

I've seen highs. Lately it's been lows. My storybook fell apart at the spine. Kellie and I served with four other families in Guatemala that are also now divorced. So was it worth it? From my pledge to never return here, to risk everything, to finally lose my marriage? I wish I could tell you that I didn't make mistakes, but I made colossal ones. Even so, yes, it was worth it. And if I had it to do over, I'd still take every opportunity to make this story one worth living. When Nancy suggested that we co-write about God's restorative nature, I decided to share my continued journey with God. How God has brought two unlikely co-authors together starts with Nancy's story.

Underwater Understanding

Nancy Hulshult

I heard God underwater. He had me where He wanted me... swimming laps back and forth, no phone, no television, absolutely nothing to distract me. After I gave him thanks for the water and the privilege of access to the pool, I prayed for others, lap by lap. Then I listened for his response. During a season, my husband and I considered purchasing land, but it was more his idea of investment and a throwback to his childhood days spent exploring the creek and woods behind his house. I just went along for the ride. On a whim, my daughter-in-law, Ginny, sent us a listing of a house and said, "You should buy this." It had 21.8 acres of woods, 2 creeks, a hay field, a barn, and a pine grove that circled an inground pool, all just 15 minutes from our house. We met her and her family with four boys and started to explore the woods before the realtor arrived. Not yet seeing the inside of the house, we all fell in love with the grounds. Birds of many species flew over us, and my bird-watching grandson, Evan, could identify them all. The winding trail kept us intrigued until we found the creek that had been calling us with its rippling laughter and trickling calm. My husband was ready to bid on the land without seeing the house. Then the realtor arrived, saying that the property owners had already received an offer to purchase. We were amazed at the beauty of this piece of land and disappointed that it was already engaged to be married to someone else.

As time passed, each of my underwater meditations ended with the Lord's vision of the property. I would go home and ask my husband if he had moved on from thinking about the land. No, he searched for similar acreage, but none like this. I asked God to release me from our pining for the woods; instead he showed me a vision of the Grateful Heart Ministry and how we could draw people closer to him by immersing themselves in his peaceful nature.

We didn't own the land, but God pursued us to make a backup

offer that, if accepted, would cause us to redefine our retirement plan and financial investments beyond what others might consider to be prudent. I was excited about creating a ministry with my husband that had purpose and that would serve pastors, leaders, and families so stressed in pandemic times. The church was changing, people were isolating, schools were doing remote learning, and the world needed peace. We thought we could offer just a bit of heaven on earth to at least a few.

We decided that if we acquired the land, we could cash in funds, take tax hits that would give chunks of cash back to the government, and give up our previous plan of a golden nursing home and spoiling our 15 grandchildren.

More than a month later, it happened. We signed the offer to purchase and set about preparing the house and land as a retreat center. We underestimated costs, needs, and labor, but we cut our home budget, shopped the auction houses and accepted donations of household supplies. My husband stressed over finances, and I cringed over downsizing shopping and spoiling the grandkids. We argued, doubted ourselves, and sought guidance. In separate prayer times, God told us to relax...and to keep swimming.

The first group visited the retreat center, and I was asked to join them. We hiked and sunned and played games and laughed until we almost drowned singing hymns while playing volleyball. I looked around at the group and thought about their burdens: congestive heart failure, dementia, teen angst, grief, trauma, depression, and exhaustion. Grandparents, grandchildren, nurse, chaplain, widows, all were laughing and relaxing, some for the first time in years. In this beautiful sanctuary, I realized what God had intended for all of us...to reconnect and to be restored in spirit.

Under water, understanding, I had underestimated God.

The second group visited the retreat center for their family Christmas vacation. I had received a message from an ex-missionary,

Chad, whom I had met in Guatemala. I had written a chapter about him and his children in my first book, I'm Still Here, and had sent him a copy. Other than a message of thanks, we really didn't correspond on a regular basis. Now a crisis had brought us together again.

Chad had heard that I might have access to a place for his family to vacation between Christmas and New Year's Day. He had been responsible for the miscommunication leading to the loss of their reservation at Dollywood. His mother was upset with him, and he was drowning in guilt, needing to make everything right. However, he had been unable to book a reservation at similar resorts for his three children, his parents, and himself. He said that he understood that he might not "qualify" for a leadership retreat, as is the mission of Grateful Heart Ministry, but he would not be able to host five other people in his tiny apartment in Indiana. Seeing the need, having a vacancy, and having a heart for family gatherings during the holidays, I consented.

From this connection, we began to catch up since our two weeks together in Guatemala. From these exchanges, I realized that God had once again "connected the dots" for us to continue our friendship. There was more to this chance encounter than booking a family vacation. God was up to something, and I was intrigued to see what part I might play in his plans.

Chad was drowning in guilt about no place to host his family, and I was hearing God underwater about a place to host people for renewal. We connected and communicated.

Once again, I had underestimated God. Chad said that he had grown up in Middletown, where the retreat center was located. When I asked him the address of his childhood home, we both were surprised. His childhood home and the retreat center were just one mile apart. Chad had played in the creek that led behind the Grateful Heart grounds; and he had run through the adjacent woods; and he had thrown hedge apples at his grade school friends from the trees in the neighborhood.

As a surprise for Chad, my husband and I drove past Chad's childhood home and from the passenger's side, I filmed his house and the stretch of houses on either side. I sent him the video and waited for his response. He was shocked to see so much of the area as he had remembered. He said that his parents had sold the house and moved away when he left for the mission field. However, they were in the process of building a home in Middletown and were moving back.

What was God doing here? Was he calling Chad back to his roots? Back to his home? Something was happening beyond my comprehension, but God had my attention.

3

Never too Late to Go Home

CHAD P. SHEPHERD

The familiar sound of my Facebook Messenger app squirrel-diverted my attention away from my attempt to write. A video appeared on the screen from a trusted friend, so I pressed the play arrow. The view was clearly from a passenger window, and the first house that I saw looked deeply familiar. Could it be? I saw the old fencepost go by, and a smile exploded on my face as my childhood home appeared on my iPhone.

My dad and Grandpa Harry built that fence line that still stands on the back lot of the property. My dad, my Grandpa Carmel, and I built that front room that extends from the front of the house. My dad and I once ripped down a portion of that chain-link to the left of the garage when we'd forgotten to detach a chain before slipping the transmission of that step-side truck into Drive. I'd backed my Dodge Horizon into the house one day while my dad sat inside, hearing the collision and knowing immediately what had happened.

I'd taken a thousand three point shots on a basketball goal that was no longer there, hugged some amazing dogs, sat in a treehouse, and imagined tragedy and heroic comebacks a million times in that backyard. This was the home of my childhood, the geography of my greatest imaginations and memories of all my best friends. All of my grandparents, who are now gone, embraced me on that plot of land.

Time stood still as my heart swelled and broke with thanksgiving and loss, all rolled into a single powerful gut punch. I want to go home.

Several of you, who know me best and perhaps love me most, have recently reached out with a sincere, "Chad, how are you really doing?" If you were here to ask me this in person, you would all be met with an uncomfortably long and blank stare.

Life.

I could tell you the tough things, but at the same time I'd be internally chastising myself for focusing on the whiny negative things of my life that are either self-imposed natural consequences or positive things in my life that I tirelessly work to reframe as negative.

How am I? I'm freaking insane. I'm better than I've been in years. I'm studying and praying again. I'm writing again. I'm investing into my church and into my work with the non-profit. I'm this inexplicable mixture of saint and sinner. I'm blessing lives and uttering curses. I'm beating myself with heat and pressure into becoming a better person, and I'm probably a bit more coarse and sometimes even more offensive than the typical Sunday morning attender.

How's that? And really, how are you? How are we all, really?

Now to those who asked that question, please don't take offense. Any writer worth her or his salt knows how to write for dramatic effect. You and I are quite good, and please do not stop asking. I do need you. This is just a late night purge and attempt to bleed a little on this page.

Life for me follows one of two patterns: (1) drought and (2) flood. I have been in a seven year drought. It was like everything I touched died. Ministry... lost. Marriage... lost. Identity... lost. And like a dying man in a desert, I just kept walking. No excuses here. I have no one to blame but myself. I had an overwhelming wave that consumed me, that just drowned me in an inexplicable feeling of unease.

The past two years have been about healing. A return. A reclamation.

I'll recount this incorrectly, but the recollection I'm recording is how it felt in my soul. The sequence of events and facts are assuredly incorrect. My memory exaggerates things and my psyche adores the exaggeration. I mean, come on, any good story is worth a little color.

While living and working in Guatemala, one of the pastors, who'd been a part of my ordination (bless his kind heart), was Tim Kufeldt. I absolutely adore that man. He brought a team from his church to work alongside us there. Together we built homes and giant chicken coops. His team was extraordinary. They were absolutely a force!

Nancy Hulshult was on that team. She was a clown. I mean, for real, she was the real deal. On the same team was a man from another Central American country (I cannot remember which). His name, though, was Felix Escobar. (Editor's note: from Argentina, South America) Tim, Nancy, and Felix were life and breath to my soul. The three of them knew no obstacle. They were absolutely a force, and their combined work was evidence of the miraculous nature of the God named as "I AM."

The time came for my family to leave Guatemala for our sabbatical, a time to rest and to connect with family and our financial partners. However, the week prior to our departure, we decided to end our time in Guatemala and seek a new life back in the U.S. After our return to the States, life began to fall apart, and I lost all contact with our friends on the mission field.

But the story does not end there. There was a word being whispered yet... "reclamation."

Thanksgiving of last year found me in isolation with Caleb, my 20-year-old son. He'd been sent home from his university with an active case of COVID-19. I invited him in, and together we braved that virus and burned through Star Wars and every Avengers movie. It was a feverishly wonderful time!

That is when I received a book in the mail from Nancy. She had written a chapter about me and my family in Guatemala. She spoke of the impact and character of our children. I read those words, and I wept. I cried biblically for days. All I could see was what I had lost. We had everything. We had family. We had faith. We had guts. We were out there and we were doing it. We pushed back the gates of

Hell and reclaimed lives.

And we lost ourselves in the process. Our sacrifice was too great.

How does one recover from that? When you win countless battles and then lose the war of what matters most?

I had to breathe deeply in those days and take account of the blessings that still surrounded me. God had been good and had blessed my ex with a good man. Caleb was strong and graceful and faithful, finding a path of ministry. Aleks was tenacious and determined and was clearly finding her way with beauty and power. Sterling was growing up, possessing humor and intelligence. God was still faithful!

Meanwhile, the missions in Guatemala were still thriving. The Christian American School, Catalyst Resources International, and the fledgling Ministerios Iglesia de Dios Guatemala all were being used and blessed by God. His mission and story continued. Our work there was not in vain. We planted. God harvested. The enemy attacked. We fell. God's plan continued.

We now rebuild. We are not finished.

Nancy, the same Nancy, reached out to me via Facebook messenger, and we began a dialogue of what it would look like to co-author a book. What if we together told God's story of restoration? How he rebuilds broken and dead things. How he can bring new life where there is no hope. How he can take the clear defeat from our enemy... decimation and undeniable destruction... and somehow from that rubble grow something beautiful and new and even powerful.

I agreed to engage in the conversation. I said yes to exchanging stories and began laughing and even crying as I read her stories and saw my own truth reflected in God's interactions with her.

I do not miss the irony that I am reflecting on God's reclamation... and He is restoring me in the process.

6088 West Elkton Gifford Road, that was my home address growing up. It is about a mile from a retreat center where I've been invited to take my family this Christmas. That was the first convergence. Then there was an invitation to share there with a group, and I accepted.

Then my parents decided to move from their home in South Carolina, returning to this very same town that houses the retreat center, and that same town that held me as a wondering, imaginative, and untested young boy.

I want to go home.

Perhaps I can. I'm exploring those options now. God may very well be making a way where there was no way. He is, after all, the God of reclamation, and I am learning that it is never too late to go home.

4

†HE BEST EXPERIENCE

ALEKSANDRA SHEPHERD

While this chapter is written by Aleksandra, allow her dad to briefly set the context: *It was the first week of April in 2012. Our family was about a year away from leaving the U.S. to become full time missionaries in Guatemala. We had a great plan: we would move out of our house, live with our parents, save all our money, and then give away our stuff and leave the country. There was only one small problem; our mortgage was upside-down. We'd purchased the house at the market peak and then the terrorist attack of 9/11 devastated our nation, sank the economy, and burst the housing bubble. Our home had been devalued three times and was no longer worth the amount we'd leveraged. Since there was no way to sell, we decided to hand the matter over to God. If it was his will for us to go to Guatemala, then he would have to make the way. Although we were desperate and could see no solution, we believed that God had already given us the city (Joshua 6:2). We'd recently read* **Circle Builders** *by Mark Batterson, and we decided to walk the grounds of our property, follow the pattern of the nation of Israel marching around Jericho, and then allow God to deliver to us the victory that he already had won. By our faith, we would claim that he is able. This is that story from the eyes of Aleksandra, who was nine years old. Thank you, Aleks. I love you. —Dad*

Prologue

I have had the best experience that nobody has ever had.

I have had the best experience that you will wish you had.

This experience is a Christian experience, but even if you aren't Christian, you should still read this.

This true story will take you on one adventure, and that adventure you will never forget.

This story is a true story, a true story you will love.

This is an amazing journey you will be taken on.

Once in 2012 my dad had circled around our house six times once a day at about 9:00 at night. Then one Friday night our dad told us to come outside. He read us the battle of Jericho from his phone. Then he told us what we were going to do.

He told me to get my recorder and my brother to get his trumpet. He told us that we were having trouble selling our house, so we were going to use the story of the Battle of Jericho.

But he said, "hopefully our house won't fall down," he said in a laughing voice.

He told my mom to collect seven pebbles, because he said, "I can't keep track." So we went around the house once and my dad threw a pebble at the window. Then we went around again.

This time about halfway around, a car pulled up on the driveway and we knew right away who it was. It was our grandparents. My grandma had a bullhorn in her hand and they joined in. We went around again. And all those times we were in complete silence.

Then we went around a fourth time and a fifth time and a sixth time. Then on the seventh time when we passed through the gate, it closed. We thought it was our grandpa shutting it, but he wasn't even close.

Then at that moment, we knew God was right behind us.

Then we threw that last pebble. And then...

I blew into my recorder,
Caleb blew into his trumpet,
my grandma blew in her bullhorn,
my dad and mom screamed,
and so did my grandpa,
and my dog started barking.

It was the loudest racket you would ever hear. Our neighborhood is full of old people, and then we saw all the lights go on.

Then the next day my mom's cousin called and said that they were looking for a house.

They now live in our old house. Now we live in our grandparents' basement. It is fully furnished and very comfy.

The End.

And that is my best experience.

Thanks for reading!! :)

Footprints in the Snow

Nancy Hulshult

From our Guatemala work camp to writing about God's restorative nature, Chad and I have become friends turned family. Our writing has helped us to leave footprints about people and events that make up our collective voice and testimonies.

I have known some people for just a few moments who have left a lasting impression on me. The Guatemalan woman carried a baby on her chest, one on her back, holding the hand of her toddler, and somehow juggling a pack of scarves to sell to tourists in the city square. I don't know her name and didn't buy anything from her, but whenever I think that daily life is hard, I see her and adjust my attitude about life.

I have also known some people for a lifetime who don't impress me at all with their one dimensional world view and no awareness of their own limitations and human frailties.

Then there's this one friend for life who has left an indelible impression on me for three notable characteristics: his appreciation of music, his love for nature, and his humorous insights into human nature. Others may refer to him as a guitar player, a tree hugger, or a comedian, but I just call him my friend. Even though his career was couched in computer skills to pay his bills through retirement, he spends his weekends playing guitar with various groups and consistently with his church band. His bass singing tones and bass guitar playing have enriched praise and worship music in both white and Hispanic Catholic churches. When he is not working or strumming, he is planning his next sabbatical, which has always included an extended visit into nature: hiking snowy mountains in Canada, kayaking in the Atlantic Ocean, camping out West in beautiful national parks, or photographing the autumn colors of Vermont.

Living in different states, we find our visits short, phone calls long, and texts hilarious, including regular bits of politics, human interest stories, family updates, spiritual revelations, and plans for our next trips: mission work camps for me and nature reserves for him. I gravitate to people, while he is drawn to nature. He has a talent for nature photography and has given me several frameable photos of waterfalls, babbling brooks, trees with multi-colored leaves, snow covered mountains, fields of wildflowers, and incredible sunrises and sunsets.

Recently, he decided to sell his home near a bustling city and relocate to the northwest part of the country with access to national parks, the Canadian Rockies, fishing for salmon in nearby rivers, and kayaking the Pacific coastal waters. No longer tied to his job, he retired and quickly tired of doctors' visits, maintaining his lawn, and feeding the birds and critters in the natural environment of his backyard.

After months of painting and repairing his home, selling or donating most of his belongings, even his photography equipment, he packed a pod of furnishings and sent them off to the state of Washington. The rest of his essentials he packed into a small U-Haul trailer and pulled it behind his van, out of his driveway, and onto the highway for a five day trek to his new life for the rest of his life. With bittersweet memories in his rearview mirror, he looked forward to daily adventures absorbed in nature: nature settings of all climates and altitudes.

He stopped at our house near Hamilton, Ohio to visit with his siblings because he doubts that he will ever return to his hometown. My husband and I could see the tires of his van weighed down by last minute items shoved into every available space with glimpses of a lamp shade, three guitars in cases, and boxes of granola. We exchanged hugs and chided about his long grey beard that had grown to his chest since we had seen him last. His short-sleeved T-shirt and cargo pants signaled his plans for a comfortable trip, and assuredly a comfortable life. With my phone, I snapped a picture of him leaning against his car with his legs crossed and waving a hand in the air. He had made it this far!

After a cool drink and a catch-up chat, we ate dinner together and shared his excitement and trepidation in his temporary state of homelessness. He rested while my husband and I shopped for a lock for his hitch and for some fresh fruit for the rest of his journey. He made plans to meet with his siblings the next day and joined us for a short hike through our woods.

As we walked, we shared our love for nature and how just being in nature restores our good nature. We feel calmer, more reflective, and more appreciative of how God has blessed us. We recounted our separate vacations through various national parks and our desire to revisit as soon as possible. He was definite about his plan never to return to his home town again and said that he may probably not see his family or childhood friends again. There was too much nature to explore in his days ahead, and he wasn't looking back. He had no responsibilities of a wife or children, and his primary purpose in this stage of his life was to enjoy nature. First, he needed to find a church where he could play his bass guitar on the weekends, and secondly, he needed to find a small but functional living space to serve as home base.

With final goodbyes, prayers for safe keeping, and lingering well wishes, we waved to our friend with wistful thoughts of all the beautiful places where he would hike, fish, kayak, and play his guitar. I'd like to think that God has a special place in his heart for people who love nature and love all that he has created. There are still places on earth where no human being has personally seen or traversed. I'd like to think that God wants humans to explore the rest of his world outside the Garden of Eden.

In addition to uninhabited land, there are unexplored oceans and unexamined creatures in rainforests that are still known only to our Creator. Is he waiting for us to find them and appreciate what he has made for us to enjoy, or is he hoping that there is part of the world reserved only for his eyes and appreciation? Thankfully, God has created systems in nature that recreate themselves and restore what has been destroyed. I hope that God stays ahead of humans in this regard.

Turning back to our house and our daily routine, I came across our friend's favorite photograph from all his photos of past hikes in nature. In the distance is a series of sharp, rocky mountains, some snow capped, rising to meet a sky of azure blue. The valley between the mountains has a forest of tall, dark green pine trees that borders a trail of deep, pure snow running closely along a cliff. In this expansive scene that could only be described as "majestic", there is only one sign of human existence: a single line of footprints that belong to just one person, the photographer, my friend.

I imagine being in this picture, the only person to see these magnificent mountains from this height and this distance, that I am the first and maybe only person of the day to feel the fresh cold mountain air on my face, to inhale the sweet scent of the pine trees through my nose while blowing frosty air past my lips, to hear the crunch of my boots trudging through a crystallized blanket of snow on the trail, and to know that anything I would scream or whisper would rise to the heavens, staying just between my Creator and me.

Even a photograph of nature can inspire me, almost as much as if I were there in person and causing me to want to be there in person. I can only imagine what God has for my friend next! I imagine that God is just as excited. Nature: the supernatural revealed in the natural.

My friend's footprints left an impression in the snow and in my memory. I hope that my footprints leave an impression for someone else, perhaps only for a moment, or perhaps for eternity.

Lasting Impressions

Behold
Nature's sanctuary
A solitary set of footprints
In the pristine snow
Frozen only for a season
Capturing the heart
Of God and his creation
Sharing timeless moments
Pondering breathless beauty
A quiet sojourner
Making his own path
Through the soul
Of life-changing landscapes

Should the midday sun
Slowly melt the frozen molds
Of the sojourner's sole
Still God and creation
Yearn for his return
To the timeless sanctuary
Remembering the thoughts
And sounds
Of the solitary sojourner
Passing through
Leaving deep impressions
Of who he was
And is

Imprinting the mind
And warming the heart
Knowing the wisdom
Of pausing
To look back
On what was
And is
Should others trace the traveler's
steps
Erasing the precious portrait,

Another lifelong friend, Nancy Teepen, took a tour of the Holy Land and then followed up with a trip out West. The next chapter records her experiences of finding God in nature, both internationally and nationally.

6

WHERE I NEED TO BE

NANCY WEISBRODT TEEPEN

I have always gravitated to nature. As a child, I grew up on two wooded acres and have memories of sitting on a hillside looking out over the hills for long stretches of time. I don't remember what I thought about, but I remember how I found peace in that space. I don't always have words when I am sitting still in nature....I call it God's space. Instead, I feel drawn in and at peace. I don't always have an agenda or a set time, but rather feel a calling to get in some quiet time. I look out over my back yard and just sit.

Sometimes thinking happens, sometimes nothing happens, and that is likely the greatest gift, as my mind rarely stops. I am drawn to be outside, or at least to put my eye on God's creation. It is my restorative space. Important events and what I call "nudges" often come when I am outside.

My husband and I both enjoy being outdoors. We took a hike up Bender Hill in Cincinnati early in our relationship. Once at the top, we sat and enjoyed a view of the Ohio River down below. I knew he was a "keeper" when he asked me what I wanted to do when I retired. I answered, "Travel out west."

He asked where I would want to live. I answered, "In a cabin in the woods." A knowing look passed between us and our relationship turned a corner. We both felt a nudge from God.

Not long after, we married. We found that cabin in the woods. Well, not exactly a cabin, but a house situated on a few wooded acres. There is a room that overlooks the woods. We spend our time there when the weather is harsh; otherwise, we are on the deck watching the deer and the occasional fox meander around. We have both taken to feeding the birds, and we attempt to identify the different species. The varied colors and markings amaze me.

I wish I could explain why exactly, but this space gives me a sense of peace that I don't find elsewhere. I "know" God when I am in this space. It's as if God speaks to me as the birds flit around, the deer turn and give me a look. I revel at the colors in the spring, the many shades of green that seem to shimmer and sparkle in the summer, the sunrise and sunset, so colorful in the autumn. Only a God as awesome as mine could do this, and I am gifted daily by God's presence when I sit and take it in.

We also bought a camper and visited those places out west I dreamed of, and I was not disappointed. It was God's playground. Imagine it, and God has created it. We hiked to the heights and marveled at the immenseness of this world. We enjoyed the beauty of the hills and rocks, seeing all the colors of the rainbow in the sand. I questioned park rangers to understand how these colors came about, but I finally accepted it as just God's palette for us to enjoy. Many times I caught myself and just stopped to breathe it all in, to try to contain the joy that I felt. Our God is an awesome God.

One more item on our bucket list was Israel. A group from our church was going for 10 days to be immersed in the land, the culture, and the history of Jesus' time. I wanted to experience this, but the journey made me apprehensive as I am not a fan of long flights and closed spaces. Our entire journey was 21 hours, from stepping out of Cincinnati to stepping into Israel. I was not at all sure how I would handle that stress but decided to put it to prayer. I knew I was supposed to take this journey. The trip was long but not stressful. I was blessed beyond measure for tackling my anxiety.

We arrived and began the journey across Israel. I floated in the Dead Sea, walked in the desert that Jesus spent time in, and visited Capernaum, Jesus' base during his ministry. I crossed the Sea of Galilee in a fishing boat. I climbed to Mount Olive and sat in the Garden of Gethsemane. That was my most touching moment, sitting in the same space where the apostles sat. I could look across the valley and see the path Jesus likely took while being led by the soldiers to his death. It was a beautiful space, though there was sparse vegetation. The trees were few and scraggly. There were boulders scattered around. I sat in this quiet, peaceful space and pondered Jesus' last hours with his disciples. How could this be a place of peace knowing Jesus felt so alone here? But I did not feel alone. I felt Jesus' presence even in this barren space.

We journeyed on to Jerusalem and experienced the bustling markets.....such irony. Then it was time to head back home, 21 more hours back to Cincinnati. Every day we walked, hiked, climbed, and enjoyed the landscape of beautiful, but very different terrain. I will never be the same. Walking where Jesus walked, experiencing the land, the climate, the ruins, the vegetation, God gifted me with a serene sense of peace. It was a life changing event for me. Jesus' presence was very profound.

I thank God every day for the many ways that he gets my attention. I am grateful for the beauty all around me. When I am missing my connection, I just need to find some place to be in nature, and there I find God at work creating more beauty for me to enjoy.

> *"Let all that I am wait quietly before God, for my hope is in him. He alone is my rock and my salvation, my fortress where I will not be shaken." —Psalms 62:5-6 (NLT)*

7

SHE IS NOT AFRAID OF THE SNOW

CHAD P. SHEPHERD

It was her fifteenth birthday. We'd spent the last four years living in Guatemala and Aleks had watched her friends turn fifteen with giant quinceañeras, the traditional celebration of a girl growing into a young lady. Aleks had dreamed of having her own quinceañera, and I was so sad that our work in Guatemala, while fully worthwhile, returned us to the U.S. flat broke. Her mother saved the day, arranging a night at a local dinner theater. Aleks carried herself with a grace beyond her 15 years that evening. I remember sitting at that table as if I were still there.

In the contour of her face I see her character. Spirited eyes above cheekbones wink with a vivacious view of a life meant to be caught. The line of her mouth can temper the emotion of an entire room with a mere upturn or frown. A resilient tenacity dares anyone to cross her and is set in the silhouette of her jawline and neck. "She is clothed with strength and dignity, and she laughs without fear of the future." —Proverbs 31:25 (NLT)

Raspberry drizzled cheesecake on white china reminds me of another so dear to my primal heart. I close my eyes in the dim light and smile as I ever so faintly hear the warm memory of her laugh. My soul is warmed to a shiver as I realize that the universe has placed the best parts of my beloved Mamaw deep in the being of my daughter.

A calm peace covers my mind as the chaos and noise that often dominate my thoughts are gone as if covered by a thick blanket of freshly fallen snow. The crimson of the raspberry sauce fills my tastes and covers my senses. This moment is sealed in memory as one of those eternally captured snow-globe panoramas of reminiscence.

Reaching back in my mind, I see a snow covered day with my Mamaw Ruth filled with a plastic disc sled, a bounding golden retriever, a risky road-trip adventure to Wendy's and the warmth of loving what the day could offer with her. She opened my eyes to the beauty found in every day of living. She covered the mundane bleakness of life with crashing waves of fierce crimson, dished out as drizzled cheesecake, laughter, and kisses. "She has no fear of the winter for her household..." —Proverbs 31:21 (NLT)

I look up to the face of my daughter, Aleks. I am amazed by her ability to laugh and find beauty in all circumstances. I watch her movements as candles reflect on her face. Strength and dignity are her clothing, and she laughs at the times to come.

I nearly weep with the realization that my life is so richly blessed by these two women of virtue, my daughter and my grandmother.

Mamaw Ruth & Sterling

8

THE MASTER SKIPPER

NANCY HULSHULT

Skipping rocks across water is a family tradition...and a learned skill. My dad was the best at skipping rocks far into the middle of a lake, maybe 10 skips or more, or across a creek to the dry bank on the other side, clacking on the other rocks. For hours on summer afternoons, we scanned the shores looking for flat rocks that would fit into the palms of our hands. Dad skipped all sizes of rocks, some almost oval shaped. Usually the best we could do was skip our rocks once, maybe twice until they disappeared into the water. When we thought we had found and thrown all the flat rocks, Dad kept going. He was the Master Skipper! Only when we gave up did we stop to ask Dad his secret to skipping rocks.

With a calm voice and great patience, he showed us how to curl our index fingers around the edge of a smooth stone and secure the other end with our thumbs. He showed us how to flick our wrists back and arc our hands to be horizontal with the surface of the water. The more power we used to fling the rocks, the farther they flew and the more skips they took. We learned that the secret wasn't finding perfectly flat rocks; it was knowing what to do with them, how to turn heavy non-floating objects on the shore into flying missiles across the water. The secret was not in the basic nature of the stone; it was in the person who gave it the power to change its trajectory...to fly, to dance across the water, to do the seemingly impossible. I guess that was the fascination: turning a rock into a rocket. As we practiced, we got better and counted our skips until they were too fast and too many to count.

As grandparents, when we take our grandkids to the water's edge, we enjoy watching them search for perfectly flat stones, watching them kerplunk the stones in the deep water, and wait for them to ask us our secret to skipping rocks.

We also love to tell them about Peter from the Bible, the man Jesus called the Rock, the disciple who thought he could imitate

Jesus by walking on water before learning his Master's secret to defying the basic laws of nature...using his power and faith to do the impossible. Peter had faith enough to follow Jesus on the water. He just needed more faith and lessons that helped him to more skillfully follow in his Master's footsteps. Eventually, Peter learned to tap into his new power that would fascinate others, that would get their attention, to do what seemed to be the impossible, and to teach them what the Master had taught him. Peter is the Rock who sank in the water from not knowing the secret of the transfer of power: faith in his Master, Jesus Christ.

9

"Well, You Sure Aren't Jesus Christ!"

CHAD P. SHEPHERD

My mother's pointed response silenced me. She had concerns about my safety in Guatemala, and I had been giving her doses of Paul. "To live is Christ and to die is gain" really wasn't helping her as I quoted it. She knew enough Bible to tell me she didn't need her child quoting it at her. She said that she shouldn't have to endure watching us go through hard times or see us in danger. I made the fatal error of stating, "Even Mary, the mother of the Son of God, had to watch her son suffer. Why should you expect to have it any better?"

That's when she hit me with, "Well, you sure aren't Jesus Christ."

I know that to be oh-so-true. Life has demands, and God has given me a calling. Living in the Kingdom of God means that the stuff of the world has to be yielded over. Fully. Completely. Daily.

So how do we let go of our stuff? For the Shepherd family, it was a simple recognition that it just didn't matter. It wasn't worth missing out on the plan that God was calling us to follow. Cognitively we knew this, but living it began with a great deal of difficulty. We struggled for months about what we needed to sell or give away, realizing that we needed to reduce our possessions to what could be carried in 15 suitcases. The only way to begin was to just do it.

I passed out a large black garbage bag to each family member and kept one for myself. The instruction was simply, "Fill it up. We're each going to fill one of these every single Saturday until we're under our limit."

We have to be fools for Christ. I took a lot of criticism from family, friends, and acquaintances. We sold a few items, but most of it we gave away. We believed that our missionary journey had to begin right where we were. A tornado had ripped through Kentucky, and we made contact with a family who had lost everything. They now dine with our wedding dishes.

Giving some things away really was painful, but seeing the tears in the eyes of lives that were being restored was worth far more than a few plates in a cabinet. Author William Willimon[1] calls this "a different rationality". Yes, this is true. Once you learn the benefits of letting go, you see the great joy that is ready to be grasped with your newly open hands.

This, then, is the "why and how to be a generous giver."

Our kids are going to grow old and tell some pretty crazy stories. These stories are shaping them now, and I hope it shapes them in good ways. The day we gave away all our dishes came very suddenly. It was a phone call during dinner. We said, "Yes." There was a knock at the door within fifteen minutes. As the lady stood in our kitchen and Kellie was boxing up dishes, I was in the dining room shoving my children's food from the nice plates onto paper plates. To say I had their attention is an understatement.

We learned something that day: the why and how to be a generous giver simply is not something we choose. It is who we are. We don't get to pick the most convenient time or the least important items to our days. We are called to be obedient when the need is in front of us. God's timing isn't our timing, but it is always the right timing.

Recently I read the Methodist rite of ordination and I am blown away by the required responses. "I do so trust," "I do so believe and confess," "I am so persuaded, by God's grace," and "I will, God being my helper." This really is it. Stewardship is not what we do; it is who we are. I do so trust, believe, confess, am persuaded, that my identity is wrapped up in the following of the Son of God, and so, I will live it out, by the power of the one who has saved me.

My mama was right. I'm not Jesus Christ. He is the one who has chosen me.

[1] *Willimon, William. Calling and Character: Virtues of the Ordained Life. (Nashville, Abingdon Press) 2000.*

10

A Plan for It All

TYLER GREEN

Genesis 1:1 (KJV): "In the beginning God created the heaven and the earth."

In the beginning God created all that we see: every planet, person, animal, and blade of grass. There isn't any of it that was created by accident. Everything that God has created teaches us of his love, power, and creativity. Everything created with a purpose and with a plan. This aspect of God's nature can be lost on us. We view the world and the things in it through the lens of our experiences. Our limited knowledge doesn't always allow us to see God's eternal plan. Isaiah 55:8 (KJV): "For my thoughts are not your thoughts, neither are your ways my ways, saith the LORD." When we look at people, and places, we can be certain that God had a plan for each thing when he created it. I have experienced this truth many times throughout my life.

When I accepted the position of Lead Pastor at the church where I serve, I began praying that God would open opportunities for our ministry to bless our community. I knew that for this to happen, we would need community partners that shared our passion for people. As an answer to this prayer, God introduced us to the principal of one of our local freshman schools. Nancy Hulshult quickly became our most trusted community partner. We shared the same passion for young people and wanted to make a difference. Can I encourage you not to overlook moments like this? Don't dismiss what God has ordained as just coincidence. I don't believe God works through coincidence. God is much bigger than that. God puts us exactly where he wants us, and in this moment, he brought us together to share our stories with others. Mine starts in Nicaragua.

I had a moment alone in an avocado field in Nicaragua. That few minutes with God sticks out in my mind in what had been a whirlwind of a few days. God had shut multiple doors in leading me to this place. I could hear our missionary partners talking to leaders from our church, everyone dreaming about what God would do at this spot in the world in the coming years. This trip was one of many that we had taken. We would only be in the country for two days this time, flying thousands of miles from home just to look at an avocado field.

To understand the importance of this time and place is to understand our dream to provide education to the poorest kids in an already poor area. We prayed that God would provide a way to build a school named the Oasis of Grace Christian Academy, a school where kids would be fed, given a quality education, and taught about the love of Jesus. Years before, God had placed this dream in the heart of Jason Rogers, our missionary partner. Through prayer, God had provided the partnership to make a dream like this possible. That led us to this avocado field. It was here that we believed God would provide for a school.

I have taken multiple trips to this field in the last few years. Now, instead of leaders talking, there are kids laughing and singing. The avocado field is now a soccer field and a grey building with almost one hundred kids filling classrooms with more rooms to be filled in the future. God keeps expanding the dream by opening doors for well-drilling operations, trade schools, and sustainable farming. God provided an avocado field and is using it to change the lives of those he loves, and I got a front row seat to what is possible when God starts to move.

In the beginning God created an avocado field. That piece of property exists only because God willed it into existence. When God created it, He knew that one day a school would stand there. He knew of the children whose lives would be changed because of what they would learn there. He knew of the young boy that would stop a teacher to ask, "How can I ask Jesus to forgive my sins?" Before God spoke this piece of earth into existence, he knew its purpose.

We can celebrate this because it means that God does everything for a reason. He makes no mistakes. God ordains meetings, relationships, and places to be used for his purposes. God is never surprised or caught off-guard by what the future brings. God has a purpose for an avocado field in Nicaragua. When we start working with God, we get to watch God show up and show off. There is nothing better than knowing that you get to play a small part in a plan God had before he spoke the world into existence.

What if this truth doesn't only apply to a field but is true for people as well? What if there is no such thing as an unplanned pregnancy? It might be a pregnancy that isn't planned by us, but is part of God's plan. What if every person has a purpose? What if a person's value isn't found in what they produce but in the One who created them? This type of thinking fundamentally changes how we view those around us. Rich or poor...it doesn't matter to Jesus. Tall or short...it doesn't matter to Jesus. Cute or...well, you get the point. It just doesn't matter to Jesus.

We exist because God created each of us with a purpose. His plan for our lives isn't limited by our understanding. With his limitless power and creativity, God will take what he has provided and do something special if we place it back in his hands.

The Oasis of Grace Christian Academy is a perfect example of what happens when we place something in God's hands. I watched this happen. My friend Cliff asked me to take him to Nicaragua. He felt a burden to get involved in the mission's program at our church. He has a background in construction and wanted to help build something for Jesus. We sat in an airport in some city that I have long forgotten. While drinking a coffee he said something to me that I will remember forever. "I have built things my entire life. Now I want to help build something that will matter after I'm gone." Cliff has been instrumental in helping oversee the construction of the school. He has fallen in love with the people of Nicaragua and the school project. I like to believe that through this process, it has also deepened his love and commitment for Jesus. Cliff placed in God's hands his gifting, experience, and availability.

Cliff looks just like Santa Claus. The kids in the school know him. Santa tends to stand out in a Central American country with his white beard. In December of 2019 we got off a plane in Managua. Before we walked out of the airport, Cliff pulled a Santa hat out of his bookbag. I thought he was going to cause car wrecks as we walked across the street! "Papa Noel! Papa Noel!" The kids in the Oasis of Grace Christian Academy know him by another name. They call him "Santa Cliff" and run over to hug him. I have learned a lot from my trips with Cliff. I have been challenged to place what God has entrusted to me back into God's hands.

I believe that there is a tendency to try and hold on to what is "mine": my time, talents, and treasures. If I can hold on to them, I may be able to protect "my stuff." If that is what we do, we will never get to witness God transform an avocado field into a school. We won't get to experience God taking what we placed back into his hands to make a difference in the life of other people. Once we experience things like this, it becomes addicting. We won't be able to give things over to Jesus quickly enough. If God can take a field and a construction guy to produce a life-changing school, what can he do with us?

One of my closest friends was a man named Rocky Antinore. In many ways, Rocky was a pastor's nightmare. If Rocky was given a rule, he couldn't help but break it. Rocky would pay for his cell phone on a monthly plan and would always wait to pay the bill the day after they shut his phone off. I asked him why he didn't pay it before it was shut off. He told me, "I don't like them telling me what to do." Missing a front tooth from a childhood accident, Rocky never felt the need to get it replaced. One day Rocky told me that God had called him to reach Muslim people for Jesus in Kosovo.

As any good pastor would do, I tried to explain to him why he was not going to Kosovo. I loved Rocky, and I would struggle to support him. He had barely gotten his GED; he had no biblical education; he was divorced; he had no affiliation with a mission's board; and he had no plan, experience, or team. Rocky just wanted to move to Kosovo and tell people about Jesus. He needed God to provide for him the right missionary partners to help support that vision.

Six months later, Rocky had raised his support and was moving to Kosovo. God was going to take what Rocky had to offer and make a difference. Rocky moved to Kosovo for six months and served Jesus. When he returned, he was certain that God wanted him to live there for the rest of his life. For three years, Rocky lived with my family as he raised support, learned the language, and put his plan together. Eventually Rocky moved to Kosovo permanently. He sold every possession he had. He packed two duffel bags and moved across the world. One duffel bag was filled with Bibles.

Rocky used his background as a glazer to start a ministry where he would teach people a skill while mentoring them in the hopes of introducing them to Jesus. Rocky was told that if he started a church with more than ten people, he would be killed. His response, "I guess I'll have to start a lot of churches with ten people." Rocky called me one day to tell me that he was moving home. To say I was shocked would be an understatement. I have never known anyone that was as certain about his calling as Rocky was. In fact, he had just led his first person to Jesus. A young woman had placed her faith in Jesus. Now he was ready to move back to the United States. He told me that God had confirmed in his heart that his time in Kosovo was over. It was time to go home.

My wife and I got Rocky's room ready, believing he would need a place to stay until he got back on his feet. A week later we learned that Rocky had died of a massive heart attack while push mowing a widow's yard. Rocky was right. God had called him home. It just wasn't the home that we were all thinking of. Rocky's life made a difference for the Kingdom of God.

God does nothing by accident. He is never caught off guard by anything. He has a plan and a purpose for every life. We may not be able to see the plan, but God really does know what he is doing. He can take a field and build a school. He can take a man who builds buildings and use him to build the Kingdom. He can take an uneducated man with a background filled with brokenness and reach people in Kosovo. I learned something powerful from Rocky. Don't limit what God will do when someone simply says "yes" to what God is asking them to do.

I wonder how the world would be changed if those of us who know him started placing our time, talents, and treasures back in his hands? Years have gone by since I first stood in that avocado field. I am left dreaming of the next time God will give me an opportunity to place something else back in his hand.

11

RECLAIMING WHAT
IS HIS

NANCY HULSHULT

In our deep woods, we watch all the ways that nature reclaims and uses what dies, what falls, what decays. I see this lesson as God reclaiming all that is His, even what changes in composition. In our conversations about God's restorative power, Chad Shepherd recounts this sacred space in his memory: "I found it as a teenage boy. My grandparents owned 13 acres. A creek ran through it and there was a tree that had fallen from one steep bank to another. I'd carefully walk out onto the middle. With the water running underneath me, I sat still and quiet until the forest forgot that I was there. The birds would return, chipmunks and squirrels, one time even a deer. I would go there to somehow catch up with myself and truly become restored at a very deep level."

I had a similar experience. In the creek at Hueston Woods, my husband and I were with our three rambunctious boys exploring, and I was exhausted. I sat on a rock in the middle of the creek, rested my back on a boulder, and listened to the water flow under my feet. I looked up and watched the leaves dance and flow from the treetops to the water and continue floating downstream, but just one at a time. I pondered the passing of time and thanked God that he displayed this dance of the leaves just for me. When the dance paused, I heard the return of the boys to my spot, and I returned to my role as mother, renewed and refreshed. I still see that in my memory and feel that sense of renewal in nature.

Our forester friend recommends that we fell several trees to allow more trees to mature, to get more sunlight available only through the forest canopy. A few trees have to die so that others may live and grow to be mature trees to become part of the canopy that shelters the life below. The concept of pruning to improve the health of a plant is another example of reclamation of life. In our woods we have to cut down and eradicate invasive species, such as honeysuckle (which looks beautiful and produces yellow flowers with sweet nectar). Otherwise, they will take over the woods and choke out other desirable species of life. Reclamation and restoration can be a long and painful process, but the outcome is life, more abundant life.

Chad reminds us that "In Genesis, chapter one, where it describes how God created, there are two different Hebrew words used. One is created from nothing, which is used with the initial creation sequence of God speaking all things into being. The second has a meaning of being created from things already in existence, reclamation perhaps, and it is used when God further created, forming and separating the earth. God has been in the reclamation business since the very origins of everything and everyone. Chad says that "the coming of Jesus on this earth was the ultimate declaration that God was back to reclaim what was His, starting with the multitude of heavenly hosts proclaiming 'Glory to God in the highest.' Now that's an entrance!"

In Matthew chapter 24:30-31 (NIV), Jesus said that he will come again to reclaim us to heaven. "Then will appear the sign of the Son of Man in heaven. And then all the peoples of the earth will mourn when they see the Son of Man coming on the clouds of heaven, with power and great glory. And he will send his angels with a loud trumpet call, and they will gather his elect from the four winds, from one end of the heavens to the other."

Again in the book of Revelation, we read the account of Jesus coming on the cloud to take us home. This account should sound familiar to us all. As Chad says, "Every story in the bible is a retelling of this same story. Every epic movie is this same story. From Star Wars to the Lord of the Rings, to Marvel superhero movies... over and over and over humanity soothes itself with the story of goodness smashed, humanity destroyed, and the hero who comes back against all odds and at his/her very real peril, to right what is wrong and reclaim the original vision of how things ought to be."

When we feel dead, fallen, decayed, we must remember that we are still God's, and He comes to reclaim us. Prayer warriors who feel beaten or struck down must remember that our armor just needs to be pounded out from all our spiritual battles. Soon we can join the charge again. Through the process of pain, we learn mercy, grace, and forgiveness that we never thought possible, and joy will once again emerge, and we will press on.

2 Corinthians 4:9-11 (KJV) says that we may be: "...persecuted, but not forsaken; cast down, but not destroyed; always bearing about in the body the dying of the Lord Jesus, that the life also of Jesus might be made manifest in our mortal flesh."

Living in pandemic times does not mean that God is absent. He is found in the tumult and in the peace of this world. We just have to quiet our souls and our bodies to be able to feel, to see, to recognize that we are in the process of being reclaimed by him, restored by him, and renewed in his Holy Spirit.

12

†HE BACKDOOR OF HEAVEN

CHAD P. SHEPHERD

My memory of the story likely comes from my mom's retelling. I was a little guy and I was traumatized, stuck in a tree. This wasn't just any tree; it was my favorite tree in the world. It was a hickory tree that dropped nuts all over my railroad truss, triangle shaped sand-box and my tire swing. My dad had built these things for me, and he had crafted both of them with his hands, improving on their design with his own ingenuity.

A typical tire swing simply hangs with a rope tied around a discarded and worn tire. Dad's tire swing hung horizontally, creating a seat that could hold three people, supported by three ropes bolted into the tire, cinched into a single knot that was joined to the rope that was secured to the giant branch some 20 feet above the dirt ground.

Rather than a simple tire of sand, Dad had somehow gotten his hands on three railroad ties. These were the giant hewn pieces of wood that ran underneath the iron rails of the great American railroad. I suspect their acquisition had a tie to his employment with one of our nation's great steel mills, Armco.

The three ties were arranged in a triangle position, each about 6 feet in length, providing about 15.5 feet of surface area that was covered by fine sand, about 8 inches deep. My sandbox was a magical place that hosted countless galactic battles, die-cast car cities, and army man campaigns. Sometimes aliens invaded and even monsters were defeated. The good guys won every single time.

Above it all, I managed to lose my grip while climbing that tree and wedged my knee into the v-shaped juncture of the two main branches. I was a calm and independent little fella. I quietly began to work my leg back and forth so that I could free it. It was hopeless. I was stuck.

Pride was defeated, the war was ended, the aliens, soldiers, and monsters had won. I was freaking out. I began to cry out for my mom, who was inside the house about a basketball court's length away; although to my 5 year old perspective, it was an absolutely insurmountable distance! Like the epic moment in a movie when hope appears over the horizon when all hope is lost, my mother suddenly came running out of the back door of the house.

All of my bravado immediately melted into gasped tears and shattered words as I began telling her to "call dad so he can get his chainsaw and cut me out!" I was convinced that my only salvation was the architect of this magic space. The man who had created for me a tire swing that lifted me off the earth and a sandbox of limitless adventure, he was the only one who could save me.

Then there was only my mother's calm voice that took over my universe. She was consoling me, soothing me, telling me that everything was going to be okay. I was incoherent at first, continuing to insist that only my father and his chainsaw would save me, but she continued to talk and hold me. She calmed me. She held my wedged knee between the branches, and she lifted me free.

Unexpected liberation. No chainsaw. I clung to her with sobs of relief. She was the hero of the day. My entire world view shifted. The creator of that space was not my savior that day, but the one who saved me and intimately knew me. Her rescue was perfect and beyond my comprehension.

This has become a metaphor for my life. So many times there have been solutions in my own head that missed the mark. I was waiting for a chainsaw when the hero in the moment was already holding me, telling me to gently release my struggle. The rescue has already been arranged. It is not by my own struggle. It is not by my own intellect, imagination, or demand. My rescue is simply my yield, my surrender, my acceptance to the help that has already been provided and has run to me to provide my salvation.

Come unto me, all that are tired. That was the invitation to us all from a Savior some 2000 years ago. The rescue of Jesus is enough. He too was stuck on a tree, a cross, hanging there for us all. No one came to rescue him. He died there. He died there to become the rescue for us all.

He runs out the back door of Heaven, to hold you and to free you. He is the creator of this place of our imagination and our countless stories. At the climax of the story, he is the one running to free us.

Hickory nuts, sandboxes, tire swings, and heroes... my faith was built in those days.

13

"CHICK-A-DEE-DEE-DEE!"

NANCY HULSHULT

"Chickadee-dee-dee!" "Chickadee-dee-dee!" I can hear the chickadees calling from the trees. I stand completely still in the winter cold, moving only my eyes to catch a glimpse of the tiny black-capped, white bellied birds with gray wings flitting on nearby branches, seemingly trying to decide if I can be trusted. My cheeks are cold with the frosty bite in the air, but the rest of my body is protected by a hat, scarf, coat, boots, and one glove. My uncovered hand holds a small mound of wild bird seed. My arm is extended to mimic a branch, hoping for a chickadee to land on a finger or thumb. I have waited for several minutes with my family, all of us standing like tree statues on a snowy trail in Kensington Park, Michigan. No one speaks; we barely breathe as we wait in anticipation to feel the incredibly delicate feet of this wild bird on our skin.

We never know who will be trusted, and whoever is chosen as the first human bird feeder in the group feels pretty special. Today it is I. Once the first chickadee lights on my hand, takes a seed in its beak and flies away, I know that more will follow. From the corner of my eye, I can see several chickadees lining up in a nearby tree, moving from the higher to the lower branches in order, as if some silent air traffic controller were signaling their next moves as they wait their turns.

I remain still as the bond between human and bird grows, and soon the chickadees stay a little longer in my hand, sometimes taking two or three seeds. One curious chickadee cocks his black-capped head and looks at me, as if wondering why I wouldn't close my hand around him. I wouldn't dare betray the trust that has been given to me.

Another chickadee takes advantage of the food source and hops from one side of my hand to the other, choosing a different type of seed before leaving. In a millisecond, he flies off, and I can barely tell the difference when his feet are no longer holding onto my finger. I have never felt something alive so light in my hand; it is a most indescribable feeling.

As closely as I can describe this moment, I think of the space between the fingers of God and Adam in Michelangelo's painting of the creation, when the finger of God has not yet touched the tip of the finger of man. I can feel the anticipation of the two beings, not equal in power but equally involved in their connection. God's touch to Adam would breathe life into him, therefore giving life to all humankind. In some spiritual sense, I can feel the same anticipation of us humans, reaching out to feel the touch of a little chickadee's feet on our fingers. We become connected by trust, by the understanding that we are both a part of nature following nature's orders. We must stand still and provide food in a stance of safety while they fly to our hands and let us feel their lightness and look into their eyes. We are both grateful for the moment.

Soon word travels to other chickadees, who visit my family and call to other feathered friends. We are mesmerized in the moment as we catch a glimpse of a nuthatch or an occasional tufted titmouse giving us a try. The nuthatch and tufted titmouse feel much heavier in my hand, even though they are still so light to the touch. As they land, they cause my fingers to bounce slightly from the difference in their weight from the chickadees' soft touch: the difference between .36 ounce and .74 ounce, yet so delicate nonetheless.

Once the human family and bird family bond in this quiet feeding frenzy, the humans start to play with the feeding patterns. If the youngest child has not yet attracted birds to his hand, the adults drop their arms, coaxing the birds to choose the human feeders closest to the ground. When the connection is made, the youngest breaks into a big smile, and the rest of our family cheers, whispering, "Yay! He got one!" Then the oldest, my father, removes his ski cap and puts birdseed on his bald head to see if the chickadees will come. After the grandchildren laugh, the scene grows silent again, and comically, the birds try this new dining experience.

When the bird seed is gone, or when the birds are satisfied, the humans take their leave and the birds fly off to another part of the woods. The little humans twitter all the way back to the car, retelling their stories of a chickadee, or a nuthatch, or a titmouse landing in their hands. The adults are quieter, taking in the magical moments that happened in this winter wonderland of nature.

Over the years, our family's love for birds has continued through another generation with multiple trips to Kensington Park over a Thanksgiving or Christmas holiday. Our oldest grandson, Evan, has become an avid birdwatcher, going "birding" on weekends with his grandfather, "Big Paw", in local parks in Ohio. Evan and his brothers Andrew, Alex, and Joey can spot birds flying high overhead and tell me the names and physical features of the birds: the shape of their wings and the color of their heads or feathers.

Our grandsons Seth, Nathan, Asher, and Aaron study and play with a bird book that matches the sounds of the birds with their pictures. The boys mimic the songs of different birds and enjoy learning about each bird. Seth can even remember the page number with his favorite birds. He enjoys the sound of the "bob-white! bob-white!" and they all know that "chickadee-dee-dee" is MawMaw's favorite. When we take walks in the woods during the day, we look for birds and call out to them. We like to feed the ducks and geese to get a closer look at them. We like to see them dive in the water for food, walk across the ice, and squawk when other birds or people get too close to them. We especially like to watch the ducklings fall in line behind the mama duck as she leads them across the pond.

Youngest Grandbaby, Noah, has already started to repeat his version of "Cock-a-doodle-doo!" and "Quack! Quack!" for me. It won't be long before he will hear about Mawmaw's stories of the chickadees eating out of her hand.

With my bifocals and growing cataracts, my vision is limited, and I am relegated to identifying birds that come to our feeders in our backyard. Besides identifying the chickadee, nuthatch, and tufted titmouse, I have expanded my identification of birds to include woodpeckers, finches, blue jays, cardinals, grackles, and mourning doves, although there are many more.

When we became curators of a retreat house, I heard that the former owner was able to feed chickadees from his hand on occasion after trying for several years. Often I can be found sitting on the back deck with bird seed in my hands and waiting for a chickadee to trust me once again.

So far, only a couple of chickadees have stopped to take notice of me on a nearby railing. One has even landed on the feeder and eaten while watching me. The finches wait in the branches overhead until I am gone, and the larger blue jays and cardinals swoop low toward the feeders but fly off when they see the human. I am hopeful that, over time, maybe on a snowy day when their other options are limited, a chickadee or two will draw close and land in my hand. Until then, the anticipation leaves me breathless.

Chickadees give me practice in learning how to be still, to wait on God's blessing, to be in awe. "Be still and know that I am God," (Psalms 46:10 NIV)

14

Native at Heart

CHAD P. SHEPHERD

She held an earthworm in her hands with a smile on her face, that small life held in her hands. She adored it. Her brother looked towards her, capturing the moment in his own memory as he held an eagle feather. We were all part of a fellowship of Native Americans and white people of European descent, walking the land and learning the history. This was a day of sharing deep history and bearing witness to tangible artifacts in the land. And yet... it was my 10-year-old daughter who best experienced the day.

Our Native American guide walked over to Sterling and observed the cradled night-crawler in her hands. He asked her if she had ever seen a salamander. Her face quickened as she said, "No." He flipped a log and deftly swept up the mud-puppy. He extended his hand towards her and she quickly laid the night-crawler to the earth and held her open hand towards him. The four-legged little creature slipped from his hand to hers.

I was enraptured with the moment. A descendant from Native American braves and a little girl adopted from China. History intersecting history, converging here in a moment shared with a lizard thing. She immediately asked me if it was a boy or a girl. My intellect failed me as I responded, "I don't know."

She carried the little fella (he looked like a boy) until we came to a barbed wire fence that we needed to cross and then she set him down. It must have been the journey of his life! Now the little mud-puppy fella was a stranger in a new land.

How often I have felt that way in my own life. Suddenly everything somehow shifts and I find myself in a new place. This, of course, was not the case for Sterling. She was off exploring the woods around her, running ahead of our guide and being called back by the sound of my voice.

Sterling was perhaps our soul-leader for the moment, and we only subconsciously understood. She was leading us to be engaged in the moment... the immediate present.

The world can shift in a moment. One spoken sentence changes everything. Grandma died last night. You have to wear a mask. I don't love you anymore. Yes, I'd like to have dinner with you. The power of spoken word. It changes our entire outlook with a breath. Nuclear.

Sterling. My 10-year-old daughter. She was grounded in the moment. What can I learn here? She is fully present, probably more than any of us. Grounded in this present reality while the rest of us are overthinking everything. I am arrested while I type these letters and words. I am called back to that moment. I stand on the trail, still... and I am listening.

It is the breeze that speaks to me. There is nothing threatening on the horizon. It is cool and light and serene. This is the reality of the world that I live in, but it is not the reality that I see. Too often I am caught up in the "what-ifs" of tomorrow and the "what-onlys" of yesterday.

"Dad, is it a boy or a girl?"

I had to travel so far to be present in that specific moment. It was as if my mind had been forcibly grabbed and pulled through the worm-hole of racing thoughts and slammed down into the earth on that hillside with her little face looking up to me expecting answers.

Mudpuppies, binary questions, and a mind that means the world to me. Sterling's question put me in the right headspace for the rest of the day as together we followed the footsteps of our Native American guide and friend. I mean, how do you even tell if a mudpuppy is a boy or a girl? I only had to open my mind as Sterling had opened up her hands. She received a salamander, and I received a fresh awareness of my place in that sacred space.

She was there naturally, but for me, I had to remember again that despite the noise of our American culture, we are all created native at heart.

15

The World According to Junie

NANCY HULSHULT

My little nature girl is our caboose granddaughter, June or "Junie", as we often call her. She was born as the fourteenth into a family of 15 grandchildren who call me "Mawmaw." Junie was easy to babysit, not because she was always content, but because I had learned the secret to her comfort: the outdoors. Whenever she would cry, I would check her diaper and her feeding schedule, and with all biological needs met, the only solace for her would come from being outside. I could pat her, swing her, sing to her, walk her both inside and outside, and for sure the magic touch was always taking her outdoors. Junie loved to be in nature, either soothed by the wind, warmed by the sun, lulled by the rhythmic crickets, or refreshed by the evening air. She loved all forms of water: bath water, trickling rain, even running water from the kitchen faucet. When the weather was too cold, I could quiet Junie by running water in the kitchen sink over her toes or fingers. She was mesmerized by the sound and the feel and would forget about whatever was making her unhappy.

As a toddler, before Junie could form words, she would grab my index finger and pull me to the door, pointing outside. If I said, "You'll need your shoes before we can go out," Junie would run to the entryway and grab either sandals or sneakers and lift them for me to put them on her feet. Once we were outside, her adventures began. She became nature's explorer: stooping over to smell a flower, squatting to examine an ant, or stopping in her tracks to listen to the birds. She was in tune with all that surrounded her in nature. Even the concrete trough for the downspout became her favorite spot, her resting place. Her little legs and bottom fit exactly into the trough, and if trickles of water came from the spout, her hands would reach to feel the drops fall into her hands. It was as though the water trough were her personal sea vessel, as though she were waiting to set sail to some far off place.

Swinging on her swing set seemed to be Junie's favorite activity. If I tired of carrying her or of following her around the yard, up and down the hill, over to the fence to see the neighbor's dog, going down the slide, jumping on the trampoline, fiddling at her water table, or ringing the plastic doorbell of her playhouse over and over, I could always opt for the swing. I believe that if I let her swing for hours, she would be just as happy as kicking her soccer ball and laughing as it rolled down the hill for us to retrieve and repeat. For both of us, swinging her was the most fun with the least amount of energy expended. I loved talking to her face to face, singing to her, and playing silly games to make her laugh.

When Junie was steady enough to navigate the sidewalks and street in the cul-de-sac where she lived, all I had to do was to follow her from here to there, checking every bit of life in the neighborhood: flowers decorating mailboxes, piles of landscaping rocks, the water sewers, sticks, leaves, driveways with shiny cars, pinecones, people mowing, children in strollers, birds flying overhead, cicadas in the trees...Junie loved it all.

When cicadas invaded our world, while grownups complained about their loud humming or random landing on their clothes, Junie became their friend. On our walks, she would stop and stand hypnotized, looking up at a small tree loaded with cicadas on every branch. If we saw a dead cicada on the sidewalk, Junie would inspect it closely. When she went to pick it up, I didn't stop her. Cicada shells were my favorite outdoor entertainment when I was a child. What I didn't anticipate is that Junie loved cicadas so much that she would carry a dead one in her hand for the entire walk. I didn't care; I wanted her to be as close to nature and as safe as possible. Besides, she would turn nine or 12-years-old before she would see cicadas again. I talked to her about its red eyes, long wings, and tiny legs, but Junie needed no explanation from me. It fit perfectly in her little hand, and she carried it lovingly as her treasure from nature...until it was time to go inside.

When Junie was almost two years old and making sounds before forming words, I used our walks to teach her words. She looked down a storm sewer grate after a rain and said what sounded clearly like "water." She examined a pile of stones and picked up her favorite stone and distinctly said, "rock" several times. I heard words that sounded like "birds" and "ruff ruff" and "stick", but Pawpaw and I were most surprised when we were caught in the summer rain. I went up on the porch, but Junie wanted to feel the rain on her head. She patted her head to feel her hair getting wet, and she tapped her sneakers in little puddles. When Pawpaw said, "It's raining!" Junie acknowledged, "It's rainin'!" Spring rain or baking sun, Junie delighted in the outdoors, in nature, in the creation around her that seemed new every day...because it is, especially to Junie. When we tried to get Junie to say her new words for her mommy or daddy, she would not. I suppose to her, the words were out of context and surely made no sense to repeat for the sake of repeating. Perhaps she is not a performer; she's an explorer.

Now that Junie is two, when she tries to put on her shoes by her independent self, she also plops her hat on her head, seemingly a requirement to begin her day's adventures. Sometimes she wears it like a baseball player and sometimes like a rapper; just as long as it's on, she is ready to go! She has found ways to see the world at a faster pace. She runs swinging her arms, her bum wiggling, and her sneakers slapping the pavement. She can balance on her pink scooter with her right foot on the board and her left foot pushing her along. Junie shares her walks with her baby brother, Noah, and insists on pushing him in his stroller or in his plastic car with a long handle, all by herself. With her arms completely stretched up to the handles, Junie pushes baby Noah down the street to the stop sign, around the corner, or just around the cul-de-sac. Sometimes she stops to see something new that catches her eye, or to put Noah's pacifier back in his mouth, and sometimes to borrow his "paci" for herself.

When Junie is outside, she belongs to nature. The kingdom of nature calls to her, calms her, entertains her for hours. It is rarely her idea to go back inside her house. I think it is the God of Creation that whispers her name to come and play, to explore, to delight in all that the Creator has made for her to enjoy. The world is her personal playground, and I just get to come along for the ride.

When Junie returns to her home, she continues to explore. She likes to see what's in my purse and try on my sunglasses or swim goggles. She takes Pawpaw's hat from his head and puts it on hers. She likes to let helium balloons escape from her hands over and over to watch what happens. She loves to color, work puzzles, read books, to dance, and all the activities that little ones enjoy. She also loves to watch her favorite cartoon, "Bluey", which is, according to Wikipedia, "a Blue Heeler puppy with an abundance of energy, imagination and curiosity of the world." It is no wonder that Junie is glued to the television when "Bluey" is on. Junie is Bluey in real life, a perky little puppy of a girl with abundant energy, imagination, and curiosity of her world. However, if anyone mentions going outside or says the word "out", or says "goodbye", Junie stops whatever she is doing and heads for the door. She is ready to go! Perhaps more than any of us, she hears the Holy Spirit calling to her in Jesus' words: "Let the little children come to me, and do not hinder them, for the kingdom of God belongs to such as these," (Luke 18:16, NIV). In Junie's ears, I imagine that she hears, "Junie, come outside and do not be stopped, for my kingdom of nature belongs to you."

I love Junie's adventures in nature. I want to be like her, to have her energy, her imagination, and her curiosity. Through her eyes, I want to explore the bigger world outdoors: trees loaded with chirping birds, helicopters flying overhead, neighbors waving, lawn mowers roaring. I want to leisurely examine tiny bits of life at our feet or in our hands. I want to stoop over and listen to the rain running into the sewer. I want to watch an ant pushing a bit of leaf through the grass. I want to run fast or scooter down the street at

Junie's side. And when I am too old to run, I'll walk the distance. And when I can no longer walk, I am sure that Junie would reach her arms out to push my stroller up the street and past the stop sign, just to see what's around the next corner.

People were also bringing babies to Jesus for him to place his hands on them. When the disciples saw this, they rebuked them. But Jesus called the children to him and said, "Let the little children come to me, and do not hinder them, for the kingdom of God belongs to such as these. Truly I tell you, anyone who will not receive the kingdom of God like a little child will never enter it." —Luke 18:15-17 (NIV)

16

Subtle Wisdom
of †Rees

Chad P. Shepherd

I heard a gentle knocking at the door and realized two things: I had needlessly locked it out of habit, and Caleb was at the door first. (His sister would have been pounding it).

I turned the bolt, opened the door, and in bounced Caleb proudly and protectively holding a small tree wrapped in a paper towel and a bit of plastic wrap. In an instant my mind swept back nearly 24 years.

Arbor day, 1987, I was a buck-toothed, four-eyed fifth grader that made friends by making fart sounds and folding paper frogs. The Arbor Day folks passed out elm trees, and I remember what a great day it was. I took the tree home, and my dad helped me to plant it in the backyard. We mowed around that tree for seven years, and then I went to college. Each summer when I came home, I would walk back and measure its growth. That tree kept growing and getting taller each year, and it always brought back the memory of that day my father and I placed it in the ground.

It was a bit of a monument for me, and it still is. It was a good day for a father and son to learn about life, hard work, long-term reward, and working together on something meaningful.

I asked Caleb if I could help him to plant it, and he quickly smiled and said, "Yeah, sure." I asked him where he wanted to plant it, silently hoping he would select the backyard. Of course, that was not the case. He wanted it directly in the middle of the front lawn. I weighed in my mind the strange looking twig sticking out of the front yard against his excitement and the importance of this memory.

We geared up in our work clothes, I with my large leather gloves and spade, and Caleb with his boy-sized gloves and shovel. We stepped off the yard, selected our spot, and began tearing up the sod in the middle of my front lawn with two of my neighbors observing.

"What are you doing there?"

I replied, "Planting a tree."

He said, "And you're digging up all that good dirt?"

"Yep."

Caleb cut out the first piece of earth, and then I helped him to form the bed that would surround the tree. The neighborhood observers now grew to three retirees. I could hear them muttering to themselves as we continued to remove the earth and form our new home for the dogwood.

The time came for us to put the tree into the earth. We took off our gloves so we could feel the richness of the cool soil on our hands. Caleb carefully unwrapped the roots, and I saw him looking closely at their substance. After a moment, he held it over the ground and looked up with a smile as I took a picture.

Caleb & his tree

The neighbors suddenly stopped their conversation and caught the moment with heartfelt clarity spreading across each face. I received a silent nod from Ron as I realized this man, my friend, now thought of his own father and son.

After setting in the tree, we packed the roots and partially filled the hole with water to get the air out. Then we placed some stones. It would be the rocks that held it steady while it had time to take root.

The tree now is plainly visible as an 18" stick surrounded by a cubic yard of mulch. When I see it, I see a beautiful 30' tree that shades the front of our home and that also represents two very significant days in my life. I hope that this tree and this day can someday be a good memory for my son.

It surely always will be for me.

I get one shot at this, and I am so thankful I did not miss this moment: the subtle wisdom of trees.

Epilogue: Ten years later, Caleb and I drove past the old house. Our tree stands well over twenty feet tall. Its roots are deep and it remains solid, grounded with rocks. In much the same way, Caleb's life has been grounded. He is the rock in our family. He has served in missions in three continents; he has led teams in relief efforts, and has recently begun preaching. I asked him about the day and his face broke into a smile as we talked about planting that tiny little tree.

I am so thankful that I said "Yes" to that moment, and that we boldly placed that tree in the middle of the front yard. What had a humble beginning now towers as both a great tree and an unforgettable memory.

The Tiny Angel Oak Tree

Chad P. Shepherd

The subtropical heat tried to infiltrate the shade of that ancient wood, but the massive boughs shaded our family with a cool touch. I considered the length of my own days as measured against the passage of time that it had seen. I closed my eyes, and I swear that I could nearly hear the leaves' breath.

Angel Oak Park at John's Island, South Carolina is the home of the Angel Oak Tree. It is a hulk of a tree that spans over 17,000 square feet of ground with branches nearly reaching 200 feet in length. It is a massive 28 feet in circumference and is estimated to be up to fifteen hundred years old.

Unable to quite yet open my eyes and break the spell, I listened to the sounds of my family exploring the wonder of those wandering branches and shockingly giant leaves. Caleb and Aleks were exchanging ideas of tree houses and tire swings. Sterling was on my dad's shoulders, reaching up for the nearest branch. My mom and Kellie were softly walking through our little tribe, watching carefully for that perfect balance of forever memories made and emergency room visits avoided.

I opened my eyes and began to walk the perimeter of that herculean oak. My mind went to my Papaw Carmel, "Pop." He would have loved the strong serenity of this moment. Suddenly his voice entered my head, memories crashing through and speaking to my heart in the present. "Buck," he'd call to get my attention as his hairy arm, big as that giant oak, wrapped around my shoulders and invariably crowded my neck forward in an uncomfortable position. No one else called me Buck. Inexplicably, he referred to every one of his male children and grandchildren as Buck. None of us were named Buck, but all of us were Buck to Pop. When we were all together, the whole lot of us sons, and grandsons, he could call us all to attention with that one singular word.

In my imaginative memory, my head turned to smile at him as he spoke to me. "Buck, can you still remember Psalms One?" It was the first chapter of scripture that he'd challenged me to memorize as a young boy, a "lad" as he called me.

"Yes, Pop, I do." He nodded and smiled. His eyes then flashed that intense look that he'd get when he envisioned both the hopes and pitfalls of my future.

"Let's hear it."

I began speaking those familiar eight verses that he'd carved into the bark of my soul for decades.

"Blessed is the man that walketh not in the counsel of the ungodly, nor standeth in the way of sinners, nor sitteth in the seat of the scornful." (Psalm 1:1 KJV). Pop's Bible only spoke King James, I chuckled at the irony as we were near Charleston. I'm sure King Charles would have appreciated that as well!

Oh, how the memories then took over and flooded my perception, obscuring even that eclipse of an oak. I remember myself as a chubby little fourth-grader, standing at the pulpit of Camden Church of God and reciting that scripture, imagining myself as a great evangelist, causing thousands to run forward and find salvation. My friends made fun of me that day, but I was doing it for my Pop.

The sounds of my children brought me back from the actual past to my imaginative interchange with my late grandfather. In my head I continued to recite the verses until suddenly I stopped in realization. It was no mistake that this particular verse had sprouted into my mind.

"But his delight is in the law of the Lord; and in his law doth he meditate day and night" (v 2). Tears began to form in the corners of my eyes as I couldn't help but breathlessly speak the next verse. "And he shall be like a tree planted by the rivers of water, that bringeth forth his fruit in season; his leaf also shall not wither; and whatsoever he doeth shall prosper:" (v 3).

I was smiling now, wiping those tears from my face quickly before observers thought me to be insane. This great tree under which I reminisced was such a powerful illustration of the strength that is found in drinking deep of the living water of God. Its leaves were strong and it had prospered over the centuries, surviving drought, civilizations, conquest, drought, and nations.

"The wicked are not so, but are like the chaff [leaves] that the wind bloweth away" (v 4).

There were leaves still on the forest floor, remnants from the fall. I kicked at them, sweeping back and forth with my alternating feet as I crunched through them. Then I stopped. Like the crisp snap of a stepped on twig on a dirt path, my attention was suddenly focused on a small, singular object. There, underneath the shadow of that enormous living sentinel of time, was a bright green, three-leafed, tiny little oak sprout. I was captivated by the significance of this holy juxtaposition of the wizened, mighty oak and its tiny, fragile sprout.

The tears returned to my eyes, happy tears. There we were, my Pop and I. And there we were, my dad and I. I looked over at him with Sterling on his shoulders, and I was so enchanted by her laugh and smile as he lifted her and she reached that branch. Four generations of oak trees, making memories and casting forward-thinking remembrances here together, the whole lot of us tiny little Angel Oaks underneath the shelter of the One who planted us all.

18

THE ROCK, THE FEATHER, AND THE FLOWER

NANCY HULSHULT

Mounted around the photo of my granddaughter, Reese, are three cherished items of nature. Reese had preserved the treasures in a plastic bag and brought them to church on a Sunday morning when she was just old enough to understand the joy of giving. She announced that she had a surprise for me, gave me a big hug, and presented her gifts to me.

My little nymph of nature had preserved for me a feather, a flower, and a small rock. The small gray feather was most likely from a dove; the name of the wild flower with yellow petals escaped me; and the rock was a rose-colored, free formed stone that glittered like a gem in the tiara of a fairy princess. Each gift is a "keeper", saved especially for "MawMaw", from my own little "keeper."

In my prayer time, as I gave thanks to God for Reese and for my gifts, I realized the significance of the three treasures given to me from the Creator through Reese, my blonde-haired, blue-eyed little angel.

The dove feather is the sign of peace that comes when we soar to the heavens to feel the lift of God's breeze under our wings, the warmth of his Son in our hearts, and the freedom to be closer to him and to see the world from a higher place.

The flower is the fragrance of hope that grows abundantly, the hope that childlike faith can grasp and give away to loved ones around us. The yellow petals shine the light of hope to all who do not overlook its simplicity, all who do not rush through life bogged down by worries and fears. The delicate yellow wildflower reminds us to breathe life in – deeply and joyfully – to grasp it and share it quickly before it fades away.

The rose-colored rock is God's steady love that captivates us in a glittery hue that never changes. Of the three gifts, it is most resistant to change and pressures from the world. Peace and hope may wane for some, but God's love is forever and unchanging, rock solid, regardless of how many ways we turn it over, examine it, test it, or even toss it aside for other distractions.

To my precious Reese, thank you for the feather, the flower, and the rock. On the day you gave me these three gifts, I told you that they would be the title of a book that I shall write one day, so this is only the beginning of what may come of your generous show of love to me.

For now, I thank you for the feather, and I wish you a lifetime of peace and adventures beyond your imagination that will soar you into the heavens, so close to God that you can feel his breath on your face.

I thank you for the yellow wildflower, and I wish you the fragrance of hope and childlike faith that will last through the years for you to pass on its sweet perfume.

I thank you for the rock, and I wish you a steady, unshakable resistance to the changing world around you, and a steadfast understanding that God loves you and will always love you, no matter what comes your way. Stand firm in the knowledge of God, Jesus Christ our Savior, and the principles of God's Word in the Bible.

And I haven't dismissed the significance of my three gifts packaged in a clear plastic bag with airtight seals that keep them from being lost or damaged. I wish you a vision of God that will never be hidden from your sight and will always be protected in your memory and heart, zipped tightly to remind you that all gifts come from above to be loved, cherished, and shared with others, including your sissy, Remy Kate. You two girls are so dear to my heart.

I love you, precious Reese, my granddaughter, my little "keeper", and I wish you all the peace, hope, and love that God and I have for you. Thank you for sharing all that you are with me.

Forever loving you —MawMaw

19

Sometimes "Just Barely" is Absolutely Perfect

CHAD P. SHEPHERD

I lay in the sun, watching Sterling Mei Shepherd, forearms planted on the concrete, back arched, and feet poised over her head, holding a Scorpion pose at the Olivia Pool near sunset. Fearless. Bold. Preparing to strike this world. Almost 11-years-old, but fiercely wanting to be 18. She is my youngest and God was wise to send her to me last. This one is freaking nuclear. The way she attacks life, she is Genghis Khan, taking no prisoners, unapologetic, and she loves more than anything beating boys at their own sports. You should see her throw a spiral football. It is quite shocking. I've never seen a football thrown with such intensity. I've always told my kids that they have nothing to prove to this world, but she wholly rejects that. She is out to prove everything.

This child is the one who challenges me. On everything. She makes me rethink my philosophy on life. In the past, I saw her as a problem child. Recently... I have been enlightened to understand that THIS ONE is created and placed in my life... for such a time as this. I am learning so much from this little fission reaction. Explosive as the sun that silhouettes her perfect picture.

Today she was determined to walk on her hands from one end of the pool to the other. This is a feat that she has accomplished already, multiple times. But today it was difficult. Hmmm... not sure why.

Last evening we feasted on popcorn and Texas Roadhouse. We'd gone to the cinema and watched Jungle Cruise. Maybe her little powerhouse body was still recovering from our revelry?

Nonetheless, she was absolutely determined to complete once again that hand-stand walk from one end of the pool to the other. She'd stand on the concrete on the pool edge, flip down to her hands with her feet in the air, abdominal muscles tightened, and begin her trek, hand to the ground, moving forward. Her efforts today were failing. She'd fall to the side or roll forward, landing on her feet, never truly falling.

I watched her silently as she collapsed on the concrete. She lost her balance again. She literally sat with her hands holding her head. She looked at me and said, "Dad, this is so frustrating. I know that I can do this. Why do I keep falling?"

I am father. I am sage. I have wisdom. Ya... right, I had nothing intelligent to say in that moment. I paused. I gave the moment some space.

She looked at me and said, "I'm going to try again."

I nodded and smiled. "You can do it."

She walked back down to the far side of the pool. Her eyes met mine and we exchanged a smile. Her face then shifted. There is the warrior. I see her. That is the one who can conquer the world. She bent down, landing on her hands... feet to the sky, abs taunt, and began her forward movement.

Hand over hand. She'd move forward four or five feet, and then balance check. Sometimes she'd have to move backwards a bit as her feet balance checked or her weight shifted, but she fought. She continued to move forward. I literally held my breath. This was a battle. My daughter was fighting for progress. Each foot gained was like watching confidence grow.

She crossed the line that marked the end of the pool. She cleared the mark and collapsed across the finish line!

In a heap on the concrete, her eyes met my smile. I was sitting up on my chaise lounge, my hands were giving applause! She did it!

She said to me, "Well, Dad, I made it, just barely."

Her eyes were downcast, but I felt a giant smile erupt over my face as I spoke the words that won the day. "Sterling! That was SO AMAZING. Sometimes just barely is absolutely perfect!" It was like watching a movie, right at that last impossible moment when the hero did just enough to do the impossible!

This is definitive of my girl. My Sterling Mei. She has what it takes to shock the world, to save the day, to make everything right. Sometimes just barely is absolutely perfect.

"And who knows but that you have come to your royal position for such a time as this?"—Esther 4:14b (NIV)

> *Sterling,*
>
> *There will be a day, sometime that I cannot yet see in the future, that you read these words from me. I do not know why they will be perfectly what you need in this time, but I do know that they are perfectly stated. Whatever you're facing at this point, you have what you need. Stand firm. Draw strength from your faith and from your story. It is no mistake. You are created for this time and this space. Kick ass, child. Be bold. Hold to your faith and do it. —Dad*

20

WHERE ARE YOUR BEARS?

NANCY HULSHULT

A road trip with our eight-year-old granddaughter Remy was a trip. Period. Remy was thrilled to get to go to Gatlinburg with her grandparents and other family, and she was feeling pretty special that she was the only one to ride with us. We were looking forward to enjoying a bit of nature together.

Days ahead, Remy had planned, prepared, and packed. She packed everything. Our back seat was filled with suitcases and bags: one for clothes; one for stuffed animals, dolls and different outfits; one for snacks; and one for her ukulele that we had given her months before.

Since I enjoy playing my ukulele, I had hoped that I could teach Remy how to play and that maybe we could eventually play duets together. I did not take into consideration the creative and adventurous nature of Remy Kate. I showed her one chord on her ukulele, and she decided that she could play without instructions, and so she did...all the way from Ohio to Tennessee, Remy played her ukulele for us with and without creative chords, making up lyrics to her own melodies. It didn't matter to her that she could not play established chords or press her fingers to the strings. She strummed and hummed along, sometimes with a twang and sometimes not, keeping us musically entertained the whole way.

In anticipation of what she had heard or had seen about the Smoky Mountains, Remy made up her signature song for the trip: "Oh, Smoky Mountains, Oh, Smoky Mountains, where are your bears? Where are your bears?" We had hoped that we would spot a bear or two while we were on vacation, just for Remy's sake.

Perhaps as subliminal messages, Remy also had songs for what she wanted to do or where she wanted to eat. If she was hungry, she sang a song about that. If she had to use the restroom, she rhymed a song about having to pee. At times we joined in the song writing, which made us all laugh.

Cracker Barrel was her favorite stop, not so much for their delicious fried chicken, mashed potatoes and gravy, but for their enticing gift shop. Remy is a shopper and a fanatic when it comes to dolls. In addition to her fascination with American Girl dolls, Remy had a penchant for collections of other dolls similar to Strawberry Shortcake and her companions with names of fruit. I recall the Blueberry muffin version being on the shelf at Cracker Barrel, and Remy just needed to "check the price" to see if her blueberry friend was on sale.

Remy tried to worm her way into our hearts and our wallets, hoping to convince MawMaw and PawPaw to buy her the doll. Unfortunately for her, we were under strict orders from her parents not to buy Remy any more dolls while on vacation. We held firm to the parental rules, but not without angst. I lost count as to how many Cracker Barrel restaurants there are between Ohio and Tennessee, but I believe that we stopped at almost every one.

When we drove up the mountain to the vacation resort in Gatlinburg, we did not see any bears. When we unlocked the doors to the beautiful chalet, what we did see were nests and droppings of mice on the pillows, beds, and closets. We called the management office, and they offered to come and spray, but the place was infested, and we were not staying. This was not the type of nature that we had traveled hours to enjoy.

No other chalets were available, but Remy suggested that we call Dollywood, since that is where she had stayed with her family previously. We made the call and learned that there was one large cabin available, the only one left, that would house our whole family. With other grandbabies soon to arrive, we hurried to check the Dollywood cabin, which proved to be clean and spacious. Remy saved us with her creative thinking.

We enjoyed touring Cades Cove, driving through the mountains, walking the streets, rambling through the shops, and panning for gold. We did the touristy things that families do, but the only bear we saw on this trip was a stuffed black bear in front of a cheeky souvenir store in Pigeon Forge.

We said goodbye to the rest of the family, and we headed home, stuffing all of Remy's stuff and Remy in the back seat of the truck. Not all vacations turn out the way that we imagine. Not all trips to the Smoky Mountains include bear sightings, and we were left "singing the bear blues."

As we rode along, Remy's familiar bear song took a moody turn from anticipation to disappointment. With forlorn voices, we all sang together, "Oh, Smoky Mountains! Oh, Smoky Mountains! Where were your bears? Where were your bears?"

We worked through our disappointment by recounting all the blessings of our trip and thanked God for our time together. If you ask us or Remy about our road trip, we'll tell you that it was the best time ever. You probably won't hear details about nature or anything that happened in Gatlinburg. You'll hear us talk about Remy playing the uke and us laughing at her lyrics. You'll hear us singing the blues of the doll not purchased and the bears not seen. We went expecting to see bears, but what we saw more clearly was each other and nature's beauty as spectacular as the elusive Smoky Mountain bears.

> *"As John's disciples were leaving, Jesus began to speak to the crowd about John: 'What did you go out into the wilderness to see? A reed swayed by the wind? If not, what did you go out to see? A man dressed in fine clothes? No, those who wear fine clothes are in kings' palaces. Then what did you go out to see? A prophet? Yes, I tell you, and more than a prophet. This is the one about whom it is written:*
>
> *I will send my messenger ahead of you,who will prepare your way before you.'"* —Matthew 11:7-10 (NIV)

I love how Jesus caused John's disciples to process what they had seen and confirmed that John was a prophet and his messenger. I love his simple but powerful questions, especially "What did you go into the wilderness to see?"

Sometimes we go looking for something or someone only to discover so much more that God has for us.

> *Remy, I hope you always sing your own lyrics about life. I hope you keep strumming to your own rhythms until you get what you want out of life as the Lord leads you. I hope you stay close to God and keep praying in your own sweet sincere ways. Road trips are the best with you, but if we don't travel together anytime soon, I pray that your wilderness journeys always include God at your side. Forever loving you —MawMaw*

21

My Papaw and the Bear

CHAD P. SHEPHERD

"Did you know that bears used to have a long tail?"

"No, they didn't, Papaw!"

"Oh, sure they did! Let me tell you a story."

My Papaw Harry. The toughest man I ever knew. I reckon I was about 5 years old on that day when I sat sideways on his leg and watched him draw a picture of the full-tailed bear as he told me...

"I was coming down the side of the mountain, down the footpath on my way home from school, barefoot. There was this root that stuck out just above the trail as you rounded the bend to go down. Next to it was a pile of toenails from where everyone tripped on it. I jumped over the root (I had long-since learned to do so, since one of the toenails was mine) and rounded the bend.

"Right there in front of me, the path was blocked by this big ol' bear. He opened his mouth and growled at me, growled so loud and so strong that I felt his breath blow my hair. Without even thinking about it, I shot my arm down his throat, grabbed the inside of his tail, and I pulled that bear wrong-out-sidewards!"

(He even showed me the scars on his arm to prove it!)

"And then I pulled out my knife, and I cut off his tail. That is why, to this day, bears only have a little stump of a tail. If you don't believe me, check them out next time you are at the zoo. Those bears know that if they mess with a Shepherd, they'll get what's coming to them."

Papaw even drew me a picture of what bears used to look like with their long tails. I was spellbound. I was convinced. This man, my Papaw, had turned that ole bear wrong-out-sidewards!

As we all grow up, we yearn to discover who we are, where we came from, and what is our story in the grand story of life. I learned that Papaw fought in World War II and that he worked as a welder at Black Clausen in downtown Middletown, Ohio. I learned that

Papaw Harry, Dad & me

our family came from the hollers of Kentucky and that my dad had grown up with a brother and three sisters in a house that was heated by a big buck stove in the basement that made the floor so hot you couldn't touch it. The pump on the kitchen sink had to be thawed with water from that stove-top in the morning before you could get a drink. The walk to the outhouse on a cold winter night was thick with fear as the wind chased your feet down the path.

My family was tough. We are authentic. We found our way through the hard way. My Papaw could not be stopped by a tough life, or even by a bear. He passed life lessons down to his children and grandchildren by way of stories, much like generations of old infused value into their children.

When things get difficult in life, I remember that day, and I remember that when that ol' bear stands in your path, sometimes you have to roll up your sleeve, defy the odds, take the teeth, and pull that ole bear wrong-out-sidewards. Our scars give our lives authenticity and help us remember who we are.

I have a couple of things that I treasure from Papaw that my dad handed down to me. Each item has its own lore that I tell my own son on late evenings as the day grows quiet and the sun slips beneath the horizon. But the stories he told me, those are the most priceless things that I have, and I see the sparkle in my own son's eyes as I tell him The Story of the Bear.

For Every Bear That Ever Was There

Chad P. Shepherd

"If you go out in the woods today,
you'd better go in disguise.
If you go out in the woods today,
be in for a big surprise.
For every bear that ever was there
is going to be there today because
today's the day the teddy bears
have their picnic."

I didn't know how to comfort her. Terror seemed to be pushing on the boundaries of my consciousness. How is this world such an incredible paradox? I was twirling on my fingers the greatest contrast of my life: the assurance of God pursuing my soul and the present sting of death.

There was a God who created a perfect garden, placing humanity inside so that he could walk with them in the cool of the day. That reality was shattered when creation chose disobedience in pursuit of forbidden knowledge.

This same God chases us still. His self sacrifice to be able to walk with us in spirit. I know this all to be true.

Still I feel the sting of the consequence of that separation from God, that same separation that sent them running from that Garden in their nakedness.

I sat there beside my little Mamaw as tears streamed down her face. Today was another piece of this seemingly unending goodbye. She was married to my grandfather (Pop) for 69 years. How does she say goodbye after weathering storms and sunny days of nearly seven decades?

Her wisdom far exceeds my own. Still I find myself in that room holding her hand as she trembles with silent tears. The crowd pressing in to pay respects was unending. Her strength was not. The powerful emotions of the day were nearly too much. I was determined to be strong, and I had been. I came from afar to offer my faith. My God is in control.

Indeed He is.

We had withdrawn to give her a chance to rest. My cousin Tricia was there. She began to talk about how Mamaw used to teach us a song about bears on a picnic. I began to sing the song: "If you go out in the woods today..." It was such a rich moment! At first I felt ridiculous and childish as I sang those first few notes. Then I realized the beauty of the moment.

Mamaw had sung those words to us in times of uncertainty. She had sung those words to us as we navigated the unknown pieces of life. We sat in that quiet room, facing the silence alone as the words of that song brought back for the three of us a simple, powerful truth: we do not face the woods alone. We walk together. The God who created us to walk in the cool of the day with him also gave us one another to walk along beside.

With my arm around the back of that chrome and black wheelchair, I leaned my head against Mamaw's, and I began to softly sing the words so familiar to her: Amazing Grace, Blessed Assurance, The Old Rugged Cross, and finally, Joy Unspeakable! These hymns I grew up singing beside her and my mother in church.

I could see tears running down her face. One escaped on my own and left a trail on my cheek. I didn't wipe it away; it felt like a great treasure. I was not ashamed of singing about bears on picnics; I was not ashamed of letting a tear flow.

I was cherishing this moment of sharing this incredible thing we call life with my cousin and my Mamaw. Life is beautiful. Even the hard parts that press our sanity and get attacked by terror. I push the terror back, and I stare it directly in the face as I embrace the beauty.

We are creations of God. We are garden walkers. We are God talkers. We are hand holders with one another as we navigate this road back to God. He pursues us. I hugged my little Mamaw over and over and over as I relentlessly looked up to the face of God.

On that day, for those of us who continue to seek the face of the One who pursues us:

"every bear that ever was there
is going to be there today because -
today's the day the teddy bears
have their picnic."

The day will come when we go out in the woods, and I know I will have that picnic. We will all sing together again.

I thought I needed to comfort my Mamaw, but I realized that I just needed to love her, to sit beside her, to reflect on the promises of God...

...and his comfort found us all.

I give thanks to God!

23

REESE ISLAND

NANCY HULSHULT

One afternoon my granddaughter, five-year-old Reese, wanted to take a walk with me to one of the ponds by her house to have a picnic and to throw rocks in the water. I was ready to go with her, but I had to wait while she packed a rolling suitcase to take with her. This seemed excessive for an afternoon stroll, but she promised to take responsibility for her suitcase...and she did. I didn't know what was in the suitcase, but I imagined that she had packed a snack and a blanket. Over the "clickity-clickity" rhythm of the suitcase wheels catching each sidewalk seam, Reese and I chatted about the beautiful weather and how far it was to the pond. I asked her if the pond was part of a park or if it had a name, and she answered, "Yes, I call it 'Reese Island'!" Of course, I had forgotten that I was in the presence of royalty.

I knew that she wore princess costumes and loved all the Disney princesses, so I should have known that Reese would rule over her imaginary kingdom, however small the population or the acreage. In her mind, she owned this pond and island, and she certainly owned me. I was her subject and happy to serve.

Reese wanted to go down the hill to a landing that had a few feet of gravel, rocks, and pine cones from the trees at the brim of the hill. The pond was stagnant on the sides, but a few ducks and passing geese didn't mind stopping in for a drink and quick swim in the greenish water.

I thought that we were going to look for flat rocks to skip across the pond, but Reese didn't care about the shape or size of the rocks, whether or not they skipped or sank. She just liked hearing the sound of the rocks hitting the water. The little stones made a "bloop"; the bigger ones a "plop"; and the largest made big splashes that went "ker-plunk"!

When we tired of looking for rocks, we climbed the grassy hill to a Reese-designated spot to rest, near the trees but in the sun. The breeze cooled our faces and the sun warmed our arms and legs. She unpacked her suitcase containing several books and a few favorite stuffed animals. We read books to Reese's plush friends, who listened attentively and fixed their eyes on us until we had read every one.

My princess granddaughter was an avid reader and negotiator at age five. When we made trips to Half Price Books, our conversations started like this:

"Mawmaw, how many books can I get?"

Me: "Pick out three books from your stack of favorites."

Reese: "Oh, this is so hard! I can't decide. How about four books?"

Me: "How about two?"

Reese: "How about three?"

Me: "OK, then three it is."

Reese: "Thank you, Mawmaw."

I love shopping, reading, and talking with one of my favorite princess friends.

Reese and I talked...about nothing and about everything. I talked about when she was born and how I held her in my arms, how she is pretty and so smart today. We talked about our best friends, things that Mommy and Daddy say, our favorite books, the best foods, and foods that make us gag. With no time limits, there were no limits to what we had to share.

And we sang. She joined me in singing "You are my sunshine!" This song was sung by my mother to me and to my children, and now I sing it to my grandchildren. Other than the first chorus of "Jesus Loves Me", this is a family favorite that is guaranteed to soothe sleepy babies, and sometimes even puts adults to sleep. In fact, when my mother was near death, her grandchildren visited her bedside for the last time. Circling her bed, we quietly sang a few Jesus songs for her as she lay with her eyes closed, taking shallow breaths. Then we sang the sunshine song, and it took on a new meaning for us: "You are my sunshine! My only sunshine! You make me happy when skies are grey. You'll never know, dear,

107

how much I love you. Please don't take my sunshine away!" Mom opened her eyes, smiled at us, and sang along. I will never forget how the grandkids sang their grandmother to her heavenly sleep.

Singing with Reese on this day was another memory-making moment for me, but Reese made it even better.

With no warning or apparent provocation, Reese stood up, turned her face to the sky, raised her hands and extended her arms, and began to sing in a loud voice: "How great is our God, sing with me, how great is our God, and all will see how great, how great is our God!" (Chris Tomlin song) She was so intent in her singing that I felt compelled to stand up and join her. Our voices lifted up to the treetops and sailed over the ducks on the water. I didn't know if anyone but the ducks and stuffed animals saw us or heard us, but we didn't notice, nor did we care. We were sharing a time of worship in nature to God, a time where the supernatural joined the natural.

I realized that Reese was not just an imaginary princess; she is a princess, a daughter of King Jesus, as am I. We are both daughters and princesses in the kingdom of our Creator! Together we shared a timeless intergenerational moment in glory, knowing who we are in God's image. We both love Jesus and were moved to give honor to God the Father in the precious Holy Spirit who leads us.

I have heard songs in a Roman basilica where the music echoed from the arches to create the most heavenly sounds. I have been in a monastery tunnel of Antigua where a few singing voices sounded like a host of angels. I have wept through the most soul-filled spiritual hymns in an urban church in downtown Cincinnati. However, on that day, on Reese Island, on a hill overlooking a mossy pond with a few hungry ducks, singing to no one but to Everyone is still my favorite worship experience of all time.

24

"The Great Sleepover"

NANCY HULSHULT

"The Great Sleepover" is the title given by our grandchildren when they come to stay at our home overnight. We don't do expensive or outrageous things, but our time together is considered great by all of us. We team up for baking contests that have categories for scoring our creations: theme, taste, and creativity. Sometimes we use available items in the food pantry, and sometimes we designate specific, unusual foods to be included. Another tradition is an all out, all-over-the-house game of hide-and-seek, which works for all ages, all times of the day, and all occasions. Sometimes we play board games and usually team up for those as well. No one wants to lose alone.

A favorite tradition is PawPaw's bedtime stories. All the grandchildren pile on one bed or on the floor and each child suggests one item (sometimes two or three) for PawPaw to include in his bedtime story, from flashlights to dinosaurs to helicopters to a sock to a red pelican to a lab rat. No one knows, not even PawPaw, how the story will go until all ideas are spoken. Then PawPaw weaves them into the story, each child smiling or silently cheerings when he uses his or her idea. PawPaw's stories always begin with "once upon a time" and end with "the end", followed by applause or affirmation that he is the best storyteller ever!

The setting is always the Enchanted Forest; after all, anything can happen in a magical place. The characters are always the same: Sebastian, Frank, Sally, and their neighbor, Henry. George is a recurring name that shows up in stories as just about anything: a talking rabbit, a flying frog, an alien, or a robot. The characters always start their day in their homes; they encounter unusual sights and have surprising adventures in the forest. They always end their day in their homes, where they are safe and content.

The story characters mind their manners, such as asking for permission to go to the Enchanted Forest, including everyone who wants to go and taking enough food to share. Adults rarely go with them into the forest, but their mother is never surprised by what they tell her about their day, because she explored the Enchanted Forest when she was a child.

After PawPaw's story, all the grandchildren make prayer requests, and several offer to lead the prayer. Typically, every family member and every pet is blessed; hurting friends or personal boo-boos are listed; thanks is given to Jesus for dying on the cross for us; thanksgiving is offered to God for the day; and a request is made for a good night's sleep and a good day tomorrow. Amen. After trips to the bathroom, drinks of water, bandaids for boo-boos, medicine du jour, kisses, and hugs, adjusting doors open or closed, nightlights on or off, all are tucked in and the house grows quiet...eventually. PawPaw and MawMaw lie in their bed listening to the whispered chatter, the giggles, some footsteps back and forth. Then silence settles over the house. Morning will come soon enough with a big breakfast and a child-created agenda for the day.

Mornings or evenings, the grandchildren sometimes gather to write creative stories of their own at a desk used especially for creative writing with a drawer containing paper and writing utensils. The writing desk sits near a second story window overlooking our backwoods with the trailhead in full view. In the cedar and oak trees hang a couple of birdhouses. Near the trail is a fire ring and a decorative metal bench for cooler nights with lightning bugs (fireflies) and our own firebugs (our grandkids).

Poised between the driveway and the grass apron leading to the trail is a concrete rabbit standing on his hind legs, looking curious yet protective, as if guarding the woods. He marks the boundary line between delivery trucks and hikers, between the world of the concrete and the world of nature. Brought to our property from our parents' home when they passed, the rabbit also serves as a symbol of the past and the future.

Next to the trailhead are two sets of windchimes, one from the home of "Grammy", their great grandmother and PawPaw's mother; and one from the funeral of Great Grandpa Meyer, my father. On a windy day, the grands can hear the chimes as they collaborate for the next chapter in their stories. On a clear night, they can hear a train whistle from the tracks several miles away. From this perch have come stories from the minds and imaginations of the young people most dear to us.

What one cannot see from the window are the secret forts off the trail in the woods, one by the oldest cousins, Evan and Reese, one by younger cousins, Andrew and Remy, and a more visible "secret" alcove with a small wooden child-painted stool.

Since this collection of stories is about nature, God, and family legacies, I would be remiss if I did not include the first chapters or our grandchildren's running stories. The stories are sweeter to read in handwriting of older cousins with pencil sketches of characters by the younger cousins. The following is a taste of their storytelling documented on lined notebook paper and legal pads. The words are recorded as written, misspellings and all, because they reflect the youth and innocence of their time together at MawMaw and PawPaw's house, at the Great Sleepovers.

> 12/24/18 (updated 4/14/19)
> *Dear Reader,*
>
> *Welcome to the Hulshult writing desk! I'm so glad you're here! This desk is a magical place! All the grandchildren can sit on the rug and listen to stories and write together. Young Hulshult writers can stare out the balcony window for inspiration. With pens and pencils, (5 to be exact) and paper and legal pad, writers can write as they please! Thanks for visiting! Come again soon!*
>
> *Yours truly,*
> *Remy Kate (4th oldest grandkid)*

Chapter One (in pencil in Evan's handwriting)

It's 8:00 a.m. on a bright summer morning in July. We're studying a small mouse that we call Pipsqueak. We don't have much else to do, here in the woods. We've been here for 3 weeks, and we're practically bored to death. It's exhausting gathering pine nuts all day, too. Living here is a challenge, and an unexpected one, too. It all started on a rescue mission to save an injured deer in the Ice Mountain Woods. We were taken out in a helicopter by Joe, the head pilot at our wildlife refuge in Madison, Ohio. In our rush to get out to save the deer, we forgot to refill the fuel tank in the helicopter. We were about half a mile from the deer when the engine stopped. We were low to the ground, so the crash wasn't hard enough to hurt anyone, but our compass and GPS were broken. We landed on the shore of a river, lost, with only woods as far as we could see.

We got out and scoped the place out to see if there was a town nearby. After finding nothing, Joe went to look for help, but he never came back. That left us, Will (12), Katie (10), Rylie (14) and me, Ian (15), alone in the woods, wondering how we would survive.*

Chapter Two (in pen)

For the first 3 weeks, we have been surviving off of nuts, berries, and river water. At the moment, Will and Katie are collecting pine nuts and walnuts, while Rylie and I are trying to build a sustainable shelter and get a fire going. We, being kids, have almost no experience in surviving out in the wilderness, so it takes us twice as long to do everything. I'm just starting to arrange the sticks for the shelter when I hear a yell from the woods. "We caught a squirrel!"

It's Will. If we can get a fire going, this will be the best meal we've had since we got lost. He came running out of the woods with Katie, the limp squirrel in his hand. We took a moment of celebration and then got the squirrel on the recently started fire.

"How'd you get it?" I asked them. Will was the first to answer.

"We found an old rusty trap in the woods. We put an acorn in it, kept exploring, and on the way back, we checked the trap. Sure enough, there was a nice little squirrel in there."

For the next hour or so, we sat by the fire, enjoying ourselves and watching Pipsqueak,the mouse (who oddly follows Katie around everywhere she goes.) The shelter is now good enough and big enough to support all of us and protect us from the rain. It is tent-shaped and about 10 feet long and 5 feet deep. It's not the ideal shelter, but it'll work for now. After all, we're lost in the woods with very limited resources.

Chapter 3 (pen)

The next day, we woke up to an odd sound (pencil). Will's stomach was the noise maker. We started are morning routine when another sound arose: the snapping of sticks. We saw a deer jump off into the woods. When I started trying to build a fire later in the morning, I noticed an odd shaped rock on the ground. I picked it up and was about to throw it into the woods when I stopped myself. The rock wasn't a rock at all, it was a turtle!

We started digging a hole for George (that's what we named the turtle) and finding some food and water. From that day on, George was our pet. His favorite snack, we discovered, is pine nuts.

One week later, Will, Katie, Rylie, and I are still wondering how we are going to survive. One day, Katie found *something extraordinary in the woods. It was a boxcar from an abandoned train! Katie showed us (along with Pipsqueak) the boxcar, and we decided to move in. I suggested that we clean and fix the boxcar up. We all agreed that Katie (and Pipsqueak) and I should clean it out since Will and Rylie hate cleaning. (Rylie argued that since Katie found it, she should clean it. Will also hates cleaning.) so, Katie and I fixed the boxcar up while Will and Rylie hunted for food. From that moment on, the boxcar was our home.*

"Welcome home!" I said. (We had to bring George with us, since he's our pet.)

*Characters' names closely associated with their birth names: Will=William Andrew, Katie=Remy Kate, Rylie=Reese, and Ian=Evan.

Remy Kate 2018 5th grade, age 10 (pen)
Christmas on 28th Street

It was Christmas. Christmas Eve. Clara Marie and her older brother, Ben, were sitting on the steps of their front porch. Their father was dead and their mother was sick. Clara Marie was worried and afried. Ben spent his days now comforting Clara Marie the best he could. In the freezing, harsh weather, Christmas here on 28th Street might as well be cancled.

Clara Marie, being the little girl she is, always has hope. Ethier a lot of it or 35 bucketfulls, she always had it. Now, Clara Marie was shivering. Ben was trying to warm her. They couldn't go inside because they didn't want their mother to end up like their father. And at Christmas time! Ben stood up and said, "I'm going to check on Mother." And he went inside.

When he came back a few minutes later, Mother was with him. They sat on the steps and talked. Just talked.

About past Christmases, Father, and Father's feelings, hobbies, and belongings.

"You know," said Mother, "you children were your father's prized possessions."

"Really?" asked Clara Marie.

"Really," said Mother.

Can You Imagine?

Water that's not wet
A soccer goal with no net
A baseball without leather
A day without weather
A table without legs
A pegboard without pegs
Paint without color
Kids without a mother
Covid-19 without masks
Sloths that are fast
Can you imagine?

By Alex Hulshult
(from his personal writing notebook 2021)

25

ALONE IN A VILLAGE

CHAD P. SHEPHERD

Some people leave indelible marks on our hearts and in our memories, even if they are not born or adopted into our families.

Her brother told me that he was 10-years-old, and judging on his age, I would place her around 12. Age is hard to estimate where malnutrition runs rampant. Her hair was dark and neatly combed and her head came up only to about my elbow. She wore a green and blue skirt, hand woven in the Guatemalan tradition of intricate patterns. Her blouse was an amazing blaze of white with hand-stitched flowers around the neckline. Great care had gone into the crafting of this textile, and it was spotless.

She called my name from across the cinder-block school, and my ears heard her above the fray of 120 students at play. I turned to her and saw her running toward me as she continued to call my name... "Chad... Chad... Chad!"

Her hand locked into mine and I realized that I had to get my work gloves off. This beautiful little girl would not be made to hold a gloved hand. I remembered that my right hand was torn and bandaged and so I removed the glove of my left and then took her hand in mine. We exhausted our mutually understood words in about 10 seconds, things like: "how are you," "I am fine," and "you are pretty."

She began pulling me through the courtyard of the school, and then up the stairs to the street, and then down the street. My feet stood still as I contemplated the situation. I was an American adult male holding the hand of a young Guatemalan girl in a remote village, and we were walking together away from her school. I considered that this was not a wise situation. A passerby could see us and understandably fear the worst.

Her name was Kenya (or at least that is how it sounds to me). She is the oldest of three siblings. This past June I worked with the team that built their house. I was nearly certain that this was her, but in the back of my mind I worried that I might have her confused, and if that were the case, then I had no idea where she was leading me.

But I was nearly certain. I weighed the risk, and we went forward. We came to the end of the street and turned right, walking up the mountain. I could see the path that led to what I had hoped was her house! We walked up the dirt road, hand in hand, making sounds at the animals we passed by. We neared the path to her house. Thankfully she turned and began walking to the house. My recollection was correct.

We stepped through the trees, and I saw the house that I built. It now had curtains in the windows, a chicken coop full of chickens, and a pot simmering on their Onil stove. I called out, "Hello… is anyone here? Mercedes? This is Chad." I listened and heard only the sound of the wind in the trees.

I nervously chuckled as again I remembered that I was standing alone in a village in the mountains of Guatemala with a child that was not my own. I took a step back toward the gate.

It was at that moment that again I heard my name called out from a distance. I knew the voice even before I turned. It was Mercedes, the little girl's mother.

The first time I met Mercedes was when I was attempting to foreman the building of her home. She sat nearby and watched as I led the team to incorrectly form her first wall, and subsequently had to disassemble it twice. Now as she called out my name, I picture the perplexed look of doubt on her face on that hot June day. I remember wondering what she was thinking, probably something like, "Is that gringo really gonna build my house? It probably won't stand. I want another gringo!"

But today the house stood strong and beautiful as Mercedes made her way across her courtyard and greeted me with a firm hug. Her two boys followed behind her as we all shared a group-hug reunion. She spoke rapidly in Spanish and I only caught a few words. It was apparent that she was both surprised and very happy to see me. She was telling me how much she loved her home, how it changed the lives of her children, and how she was forever grateful.

I was speechless. I just stood there in silence.

Luckily she saved me! I heard her asking about my spouse. I couldn't believe she remembered! When I was here before, I had shared pictures of Kellie and the full family. I laughed out loud, smiled, and said, "Si, Kellie, mi esposa es aquí!" Using my spanglish and hand motions, I communicated that I would go and get her, along with Caleb, Aleksandra, and Sterling. Mercedes smiled and laughed with delight when she learned that they were all there, and I ran with Kenya's hand in mine to bring them to her house. It was incredible to realize that we had all become family.

My hands were full all day long today. I walked around Michael Jackson style with my right hand gloved and my left hand free. I held shovels, pick-axes, wheel-barrows, hammers, trowels, buckets, and backpacks. When I wasn't holding a tool, I was holding the hand of Kenya.

She and her two brothers followed my every step from about 9:30 to 5:00. I held them each nearly every free moment I had. I carried them all around Labor de Falle. We ran, we spun, we danced, we played ball. We even invented our own games.

Meanwhile, Ramero, our construction foreman, relied on me to construct the block wall that supported the hydroponics project that combined 250 live tilapia with a veggie patch. Working alongside Margaret Updyke, we hand mixed mortar and placed over 50 blocks, level and plumb, and then gave them a stucco finish. We transported two 130-pound bags of concrete, 15 wheelbarrows of sand, and seven wheelbarrows of stones down a hill, over a ditch, and up a hill to our worksite. We graded the dirt within the walls to create a base for the concrete bottom that will hold 6" of rock. The rockbed would act as the filtration system for the fish and would hold the vegetables.

This was our progress just before inserting the tank and applying stucco to the walls.

I came back that night, took out my knife and cut away the bandages from my hands. The palm of my right hand and the thumb of my left showed the evidence of my work. While we don't always have such a physical representation, it is true that the way we live our lives bears evidence.

The choices we make and how we spend our days, how we invest our time, the things we accumulate, the way others speak of us, all these things are evidence of our belief.

Today I was blown away by seeing familiar faces and thankful hearts. I was blessed to be a part of something far bigger than myself. I figure that at the end of my days, I may have the chance to look back and consider how I lived it.

I hope to have scars on my hands that remind me of the beauty of days lived like today.

He can also do a lot with you and me.

26

300 Days to Cerro Alto

Chad P. Shepherd

I didn't know how to comfort her. Terror seemed to be pushing on the boundaries of my consciousness. How is this world such an incredible paradox? I was twirling on my fingers the greatest contrast of my life: the assurance of God pursuing my soul and the present sting of death.

Kenya and Aleksandra found each other today. I had hoped that they might become friends, but I didn't want to force it. Toward the end of the day today, I walked up on these two holding hands and nearly dropped my phone in the aquaponics project as I fumbled to take a photo.

Aleks & Kenya

I have stared at this picture for over an hour. I am sitting on the patio at Mimi's House as the sky flashes and rumbles over my head. A storm is rushing in and the pounding rain on the awning now rules the night.

I am blessed to be a part of this incredible picture: a girl from an orphanage in Moscow, who speaks English, is holding hands with a girl from a village in Guatemala, who speaks Spanish. One was an orphan and the other had no home. Now they stand side by side. Aleksandra has a family, and Kenya has her own bedroom. I bear witness to the power of God's love and incredible provision that causes miracles to happen.

I learned today that the girls are nearly the same age, both will be nine in September. How incredible that their stories have merged through this adventure that God has led.

We said goodbye today to Kenya, her mother, and her two brothers along with the family we worked with this week on the aquaponics farm.

Meet Luis, his wife Thelma, and their son Andy Luis Antonio. Andy is the same age as our daughter Sterling. Maria Elvidia also lives on the property with her son Es Bin. They worked hand in hand beside us as we installed an incredibly simple and ingenious system that uses the waste of tilapia to fertilize vegetables, and the vegetable bed to filter the water for the tilapia.

Today was an incredible day of handing the keys over to two families and seeing them walk into their new homes, as well as seeing the water flow with the promise of sustainable food. Today also stands out to our family because we realize that the next time we complete a project in Guatemala, we will only need a car ride to get home. In 10 short months, we will be living here. We begin counting down 300 days now.

Our kids now have made many new friends. We have connected with six separate missionary families with whom we will serve. We have identified a house to rent and have a solid possibility of a car. We will need to find $6,000 between now and May to pay for it.

We have a clear picture of what our ministry will look like. We step forward on faith that all the necessary pieces of the puzzle will fall into place. Even if the picture doesn't look exactly like we think, we move forward knowing that God will paint it.

The house we plan to rent is large enough that we will have room for a small staff of nannies who will provide around the clock care for six orphaned baby girls.

We will be able to volunteer at the Christian Academy of Guatemala where our kids will attend. We will be a part of Journey Church Guatemala where we will worship and do life together with believers. I will also be able to work with short term mission trips to continue to build sustainable communities in the mountains of Cerro Alto.

We are so grateful to be part of Catalyst Resources International. We appreciate "muy mucho" those who are already contributing partners. It is incredible what God is doing here in this place and with so many back in the U.S.

Our day has been filled with tears of happiness, thankfulness, and the power of true belief. I have many stories to tell, but at the end of the day, it is a retelling of the only story I know.

God can do a great deal with just a few fish.

He can also do a lot with you and me.

27

The Most I've Ever Learned

Chad P. Shepherd

Surely God must shake his head when he looks at me. I learn deep... but I learn only when my heart breaks and my dignity is crushed. I see beauty where there is pain, and I want to toss away anything that doesn't come with a personal price. Yet what I need most can not be paid by me.

Every now and then He has to pick me up and shake me.

It was the end of the final day of the work week. The team was tired, covered in band-aids, and not a few faces had clean lines from the eyes over their dust covered cheeks.

Everyone was tired. Two homes had been dedicated; five children would rest heads for the first time with pillows on beds. We all were worked out and played out. We sat on a cinder block wall overlooking the school of Labor de Falla. The village had grown quiet as we all watched the dust diamonds dance in the falling rays of the evening sun.

The breeze was kind, telling us with its touch that the day's work was good. I remember inhaling and allowing the deep breath to clear my mind. It was at this moment that Mercedes came down the dirt and block slope to my left. She was carrying a wad of black garbage bags in her hand and heading for the metal drum that held the village garbage.

I felt my brow crinkle up as I realized her intention. She had no gloves, and there was no way she could lift that drum. It had no liner. I sat as the reality of the situation sank into my mind and then my heart.

For weeks I had been encouraging

Mercedes with three of her children

the children of the village to throw their garbage in the drum rather than to drop it on the ground. It never crossed my mind that someone would have to clean out that drum. It was putrid.

I looked around thinking, "Someone needs to help her!" Then I felt panicked, convicted, and assured. How can we ever claim that we are the hands and feet of God if we aren't willing to get our hands dirty? My God's hands were nailed to a cross. My God's hands reached down and pulled me up. My God's hands point to only one way.

I couldn't even look up as I stood and crossed the distance, feeling the crunch of dirt with each measured step. As I reached down into the can, Mercedes looked up and her eyes met mine. I was overwhelmed by her expression. I quickly fought back the urge for tears to fall because I knew I couldn't wipe them away.

She looked surprised, embarrassed, and maybe even slightly amused. She gave me a look that shouted, "You really don't know what you're getting into." She was right.

I started out gingerly picking things up by the corners with my index finger and thumb. And then I noticed that her small, strong, worn hands were digging in deep and pulling out great handfuls. So I pulled in my breath, steeled my resolve, and sank my hands in deeply. I could feel grim and unspeakables getting lodged in the space underneath my nails.

It was hot, nasty, and the texture was somehow both abrasive and gooey. One of the village boys ran up to help. He started to dig in and gagged. He slung his hands, debris flying off around us, and ran away.

I looked at Mercedes and shared a laugh. Then I looked down into the can and the laugh froze on my face. We had hit a new layer. Life is an amazing thing. It is everywhere. The garbage was wiggling with it. Beetles, tiny flying insects, and the unmistakable sight of maggots. People here don't really throw away meat, so my mind pieced together that the ooze under my nails must have been bits of something previously alive.

I wanted to run. I wanted to quit. I wanted to get sick. I knew that by now, everyone was watching. I stole a peek. Sure enough, Mercedes and I had the attention of the village. So what. Let them laugh. I was done.

I looked at Mercedes, this mother of three, whom I had worked beside now for two years. I watched her open the door to her new home, and I saw her daughter cry when she picked up a small teddy bear and fell on her own bed for the first time. I remembered coming back a year later and seeing that she had painted the home we had built. The chicken coup was thriving. Her children looked happier, even healthier.

I knew at that moment that nothing could force me away from that garbage. I dug in deeply. Soon we were up to our armpits, taking turns, racing to the finish.

I have pondered this moment now for over a week. I can not decipher exactly what it is that I learned in that moment. I can only tell you that it felt like a smack in the face that brought clarity to my vision. How can we stand by while others do the dirty work? How can I sit and watch while others dig in and invest?

My soul has never felt so close to God as in those moments when I yield my everything to his uncomfortable calling. I know that so many times I have held onto what is safe and given up what is eternal.

This free gift from God does indeed come at a price for us. We must yield up our desires and our agenda. We must then take up the agenda of God and boldly, with gusto, dig in armpit deep.

Paul wrote to the Colossians (ch. 3) and told them to throw off their own desires and nature like an old coat, and then to clothe themselves with things of God. I think I had to put on some new clothes: tender mercies, kindness, humility, meekness, and long-suffering.

Later that night as I dug blackness out from my nails, I thought again of the expression on Mercedes' face. Finally the tears flowed freely from my eyes as my soul began to process that glance exchanged between her and me.

It was the simple act of showing that we are in this together. There is no sitting on the sideline as a Christ follower. We either do not follow, or we sink in our hands and dig in deep.

Elbows deep in filth was what it took for me to understand. The lesson was worth learning, even if it required me to be fully submerged.

Mercedes was only cleaning a can, but my selfish heart was what really needed purified. I am honored to have my life stretched and strengthened by these lessons of reality and the incredible faith of a fearless woman in Labor de Falla.

28

A Chinchilla's Tale

Chad P. Shepherd

Luis, Brayan, Ana Lucia, Norma (Journal entry -August, 2010)

Larry turned to him and said, "Luis, you have heard me tell stories. Now why don't you tell me a story?"

Luis looked away and paused thoughtfully. He turned his eyes up toward Larry and with a sad expression said, "I do not have any stories to tell."

I remember those first few days in Guatemala with snapshot clarity. I was so far outside of what I knew that I was more than a little stunned. I had no idea what I was doing. I was convinced that I was more of a hindrance than a help. I was sure that every action I took would probably cause someone else more work to correct it. The sunlight seemed to punish me as the sweat ran down my face in a non-stop itch fest. My boots were heavy with caked earth, and my jeans were wet with dampness from lying on my head to tie rebar in the foundation trench. Those fierce little biting ants were constantly in my pants.

If I could have walked away, I may have. Tenacity was being learned by the simple reality that I had no way off that mountain, except by completing that house. And so... I just kept on lifting block. One at a time. Mud it, lay it, level it, correct it, repeat. To my wonder, the walls slowly began to rise. As our progress manifested, my spirit began to climb above my own selfish view. I began to weep as I became aware.

Of all the people at this edge on the mountain, I was the one in need of the most. I had a moment that became the inspiration for one of my first blogs as I sat collapsed in the dirt in the back corner of the site and looked up at the machete-hewn, three meter high dirt wall.

It was like a cross section of time with bits of metal, plastic, refuse, and whatever had been discarded and slowly covered by years of erosion and deposited soil. I pried a toothbrush loose from the wall and I sat there and considered the depressing, wasteful nature of time passing without meaning. I considered the incredible contrast with what we were raising right beside it: concrete walls of purpose, a home for a family. This same space that had occupied the unwanted toothbrush was now transforming from rejected waste to a cherished space of hope.

I fell down against the wall and silently wept as I realized my own life had the same capacity. I could be a timeline of waste, or I could be a shelter of hope to my wife and kids. At the end of my time, what would be the remnants in the wall of my days?

Something happened in me that day, and I began to notice the lives that surrounded me on that mountain.

Let me now tell you the story of Luis Chinchilla.

Larry, Ramero, Luis, Brayan, Chad (day one of house build)

There were five of us: Larry, Margaret, Callie, Kellie, and me. Between us, we spoke a total of nada Spanish. Our job foreman, Ramero, spoke a total of zero English. Between the two languages stood a single teenager. This house would be his own, along with his little brother, sister, and mother. Luis not only worked alongside us the entire week, but he also translated every sentence of communication between Ramero and us.

We began to learn more about Luis, a very small piece of information at a time. At first, he simply listened to us as we took turns telling him stories of our lives, our travels, our families, and answering his questions. When Larry asked him to tell us a story, and he replied that he had no story to tell, it was a sobering moment for us all.

Much of the remainder of that day was spent in silence as we worked into the evening. We were beginning to feel the toll of manual labor with concrete and cement on our 9-5 office job bodies. By this time gloves were destroyed and fingers bled. We continued to work in silence as we contemplated our physical pain, as well as the greater emotional strain of the realities that surrounded us. We realized that we could not possibly make any meaningful difference. We knew that the week would soon end, we would go home, the dust would settle, and the needs here far outweighed any help we could give.

On the drive home that night, our driver and host Edgar began to open our eyes. He told us the story of Luis.

Luis' father had abandoned his family. They had nothing left. His father had worked, but his money never made it home. Addiction and repeated bad choices had robbed him of the man he could have been. The situation had deteriorated to the point that the family had to intervene. He had become abusive, nearly ending the lives of his expecting wife and unborn child. He now had another family and left his three children and their mother with nothing but fear, pain, and bad memories. We learned that this is a very typical story of how men behave in the culture.

This young man Luis was left fatherless at this critical time in his life. When he thought about his father, he felt only resentment, anger, and abandonment. Statistically, Luis would be soon repeating this cycle. This poverty is generational. It is endless.

But this is a story of provision and convergence. This is a story of beating the odds. Edgar was more than our driver; he was also a part of Catalyst Resources International, an agency committed to breaking this cycle of hopelessness. Most importantly, Edgar was the uncle of Luis, and Edgar was pouring his own life into Luis. Edgar had stepped into the gap. As we listened to Edgar tell of Luis, we realized that Edgar was teaching Luis how to be a man.

Ramero, Edgar, and Luis completed the house after we left. That summer was nearly two years ago. Since that time, Luis has worked alongside his uncle as part of Catalyst Resources International. Luis has worked with many groups of Americans who go to Guatemala on short term missions work, and he has now helped to build homes for several families. Luis is breaking the generational cycle of poverty and hopelessness. As he works beside his uncle, he now becomes the second generation of rising beyond circumstance and beating the odds.

When I returned in the summer of 2011, I was able to see Luis in his home that bore evidence of the change in his life.

Luis & Brayan

Luis and his brother now have a quiet place to study. His little sister has a safe place to sleep at night. His mother now has a reason to hope that her children would live to be adults. Luis was a very good student even before he had a home, but now he is able to reach his full potential. Early into 2012, Luis learned that he had achieved his dream: he has been accepted to a university in the United States. He is on a full scholarship that includes room, board, and books. With his university degree in hand, Luis plans to return to Guatemala to live with his family and invest back into the economy of his beautiful homeland.

Luis has done what hundreds of thousands of Guatemalan children can not: he has broken the cycle of poverty. He has done this through a perfect collision of his own tenacity, the love of his uncle, the vehicle of Catalyst Resources International, the support of friends, and the provision of God.

Every time I look at the picture of me collapsed in the mud, fighting ants, and having my own personal crisis/breakthrough, I realize how amazing it is that I have a small part in this story. Somehow, I was given this incredible opportunity to simply be an inadequate, ill-tempered, perspective-lacking guy. who was able to lay the foundation on a piece of land, turning it from a dumping ground to a place that is now set apart, and made holy by the God of new beginnings.

Thank you, Luis. You were once a boy without a story. Now you are a man who possesses a story with no equal. You are my inspiration.

> *The stone the builders rejected has become the cornerstone; the LORD has done this,and it is marvelous in our eyes. The LORD has done it this very day; let us rejoice today and be glad. LORD, save us! LORD, grant us success! Blessed is he who comes in the name of the LORD. From the house of the LORD we bless you. The LORD is God, and he has made his light shine on us.* —Psalm 118 (NIV)

Epilogue- 2021

Luis saw his vision fulfilled, graduated from Harding University, and then went to work in the corporate world in Guatemala City. Luis said that he felt unfulfilled by what he was doing, and so he went to work as a Solution Architect for Torrent Consulting in Antigua Guatemala. During the COVID-19 pandemic, Torrent has been part of bringing needed food and supplies into the country. Even more than that, Luis gets to work in raising up leaders within his country to continue to create positive change. Torrent published an article about his work and stated that he "lives out a strongly defined Personal Why; 'To empower others to own their stories so that they see possibilities and choose a better future.'"

What a testimony! If for no other reason than this, I am so thankful that I could be in Guatemala to witness the birth of Luis' story.

29

WHO ARE THESE PEOPLE?

NANCY HULSHULT

U nnamed, married, childless, and wealthy, the woman from Shunem asked her husband for permission to host the prophet Elisha in their home whenever he would come to town. They agreed upon a rooftop room with just the essentials: a bed, a table, a chair, and a lamp. Her sense of hospitality was driven by her recognition and appreciation that Elisha was a holy man and worthy of at least the basic comforts that she could provide in her home free of charge.

Hospitality and restoration are strong themes through both the Old and New Testament, and the Shunammite woman embodies both. She recognizes God at work in the life of Elisha and she finds a way to help him to rest and recharge. It's simple, selfless, and personal. She wanted to bless him, but the story tells us that she was blessed beyond measure in her relationship with her transient guest. For her hospitality, Elisha prays for her to have a child, and when the child dies, it is Elisha who restores the child back to life.

In blessing another, she is blessed beyond measure. That is her story. A nameless woman, who sets up a Bed and Breakfast for a prophet, gives witness to a resurrection of the dead by a prophet well before Jesus comes and resurrects himself in victory over sin and death.

Her story is personal to me because her story has become mine. I share her heart for hospitality and her love for God's people and their need for restoration, mentally, physically, and spiritually. She and her husband found a spot on the roof of her home; we found a spot in nature just 10 minutes from our home. She provided a bed, a table, a chair, and a lamp. We did the same through auction warehouses and donations from friends. And just like her, we have already been blessed beyond measure.

My husband and I were able to rethink our retirement options and proceed with our vision to host pastors, missionaries, chaplains, and other holy prophets working in churches, schools, and health care. We accepted the responsibility to care for a newly renovated house with an inground pool set among pine trees, a barn, campfire rings, and hiking trails through acres of woods, creeks, and fields. The land was already home to a wide variety of birds and critters who didn't mind sharing their space with tired, restless humans. Our grandchildren tested the creeks and found them to be suitable diversions for their curious minds. Our sons and their wives confirmed that we had found a peaceful place, and our friends gathered to share our vision, called "Grateful Heart Ministry." Out of gratitude for God's free gift of grace and salvation, we wanted to provide a free space for folks to reconnect, to recharge, and to be restored to God and his amazing creation through nature.

What we didn't know is that God's plan was much bigger than our vision. After we became caretakers of the land, we learned of a Shawnee prayer wheel that was located in the deep woods. One neighbor claimed that the circle of darkened, moss-colored boulders was just a pile of rocks, and the Butler County Historical Society said that there was no evidence of Shawnee life in our area. A hike with a certified forester taught us that the rocks had to have been placed by humans, that the circle of stones was not a natural occurrence. My curiosity led me to contact a local Native American whose family owned hundreds of acres behind our land. He offered to take us through the woods and share his knowledge of Native American history as it pertained to us. We set a date for the following weekend.

He came to the retreat house where our ex-missionary and longtime pastor friend was visiting with two of his children. The first time that I met Chad and his family was on a mission trip to Guatemala. The next time we met was this weekend when we had just learned that Chad's childhood home was just a mile down the road. We knew that God was moving in surprising ways, but even more surprisingly when we listened to our new Native American friend.

We shared introductions and some fruit and vegetables before we gathered around the table. As we listened to his family's history and how this land was once occupied by Native Americans, we were moved by his reverence for tradition and respect for his father. His personal testimony of the unjust treatment of his people was as respectful and powerful as his expression of deep love for Jesus and our Creator. We sat mesmerized by our realization that we were becoming part of the local history of this land. We were an unlikely mix of generations, cultures, and experiences forming a bond through love for God, nature, and each other. We were excited to hike to the deep woods together to learn more about the Shawnee prayer wheel.

As we followed our new friend through the woods, I thought about all the prayers for hundreds of years that had been lifted up to the Great Spirit from this one special spot in nature. I know that God hears all of our prayers that are timeless, as is he, and I felt at one with nature, one with God, one with our small band of discoverers, and one with the Shawnee: all of us connected by the Creator through his Creations. Who were these prayer warriors who shared this land and this holy space?

Before we came to the holy space, our friend stopped at a single black elliptically shaped boulder lying on the ground next to the trail. He pointed to it and said that an archeologist had identified it as the grave marker for a pioneer. I was shocked to learn that yet another nameless person was buried on this land; another family of another culture had occupied this living space and died there. Who was this pioneer, and what was his or her story that is yet untold?

Off the trail and through some underbrush, we came to the circle of stones, where a small maple tree with a small branch of leaves had sprouted from the center. Our Native American friend recounted that one center stone was missing, a squared rock that presumably had indicated directions of north, south, east, and west.

When it was taken by someone in his family for safekeeping, the tree took its place. When I asked if we should cut down the tree to keep it from dislodging the rocks, he said that the tree would actually preserve the prayer wheel by growing strong roots that would hold the soil and rocks in place.

As I took in the scene of this unlikely group of Christian people and the circle of rocks surrounding the tree, I thought of Jesus proclaiming his church on earth. Before Jesus would be crucified on a tree, he said in Matthew 16:18 (ESV), "And I tell you, you are Peter, and on this rock I will build My church, and the gates of hell will not prevail against it." I saw the circle of rocks representing us as the church. I saw Jesus as the tree in the center, leading us to the heavens yet putting his solid foundation of roots in the earth to support us and to protect us from sliding away when the storms come.

I was jolted back to reality as our friend began the Native American purification rite before going to prayer. He lit a fire of sage and used an eagle's feather to fan the smoke over us with special attention to purifying our shoes, our former steps, as we were standing on holy ground. He began to beat the drum and lifted his eyes to the canopy of the woods, I was taken by his focus on the One to Whom he prayed. His powerful voice filled the silence of the woods as he sang in his native tongue. When his granddaughter joined him with the same passion and power of the song, I was moved to tears, feeling the Spirit moving among us. When he prayed in English, he prayed for us, for our new friendship, for answers to his prayers, and for the miracles and healings that were happening in our midst. We added our own prayers to the circle, mine expressed mostly in streams of tears, and in that moment I knew that each of us was experiencing a healing, an answer from God, in our own ways.

I feel renewed, restored, and ready to fulfill the purpose that was given to my husband and to me: to be the conduits for people to be restored by God through nature. I feel the huge responsibility to protect and preserve this holy and historical space, to tell the story of the nameless people who built the prayer wheel and prayer to the Great One, and to find out more about the nameless pioneer buried on this land. Who are these people?

One day we will be among the nameless people who once walked this land and prayed to our Creator. We will share namelessness with the Shunammite woman and others who are a part of God's story of restoration. However, there is One who knows our names, the same One who has called us to be his and to be saved through his Son Jesus Christ, the One who restores us when we fall away, and the One who has our names in his book of Life.

Our purified, refreshed, and restored group of friends hiked out of the woods as family to go our separate ways with hopes of gathering again soon. As we left our footprints on the land, we were more aware of the footprints made before us. Now we carry these nameless ones with us.

30

Stay Strong

Nancy Hulshult

Our group of nine was a mix of old and young, family and friends, European whites and Native Americans. We had been invited by our new Native American neighbor, Mark Banks, to visit the 200 acres of land located behind our retreat center. The land had been in the same family for decades. Sixty-year-old Mark was proud of his heritage and happy to share the folklore and traditions of his culture. He had invited Chad, his children, and my family to tour his family's property where folks gather for presentations and representations of the Native American culture. Mark showed us a gravesite, a naming circle, and a prayer wheel, and a small wooden cabin.

As we entered the one-room cabin, our eyes adjusted from the bright sunlight outside to the obscure view provided by one sunbeam shining through the window. Partially illuminated and scattered around the edges of the room were Native American artifacts: a small handmade wooden chair, a large drum, pots, pottery, and other articles made from resources found in nature. We felt the hard rock floor under our feet and stood in a circle, listening to some of the folklore inspired by this place. We smelled the musky remains of some animal that had taken shelter in the corner of this one-room domicile once used by people decades ago.

Our attention turned to the young round-faced boy with jet black hair seated on a long wooden bench along the wall and beating the large drum in the center of the cabin. The drum was covered in tanned animal hide stretched tightly with leather cords running in diagonal patterns down the sides to the leather covering underneath. The gray-haired, ponytailed grandfather pulled up a chair made of wood with a woven seat and picked up a drum stick with ends covered in padded leather material. He asked, "Do you want to play the drum? Do you want to play a song?" to which the grandson responded, "I want to play a song. I want your drum!" The grandfather offered, "Oh, you want to trade?" and the two switched drumsticks, which appeared to me to be exactly the same. It seemed to be important to the boy to use the instrument held by his grandfather's hands. They began to beat the drum and sing in their native language.

The grandfather later explained that the drum represents the "heartbeat of all living things" on Mother Earth; the heartbeat is the first and last sound that we hear in life.

Sitting side by side, they beat a steady rhythm and sang, the old man in deep powerful tones and the toddler in pure, high-pitched notes. The grandfather's eyes remained focused on the drum with an occasional glance of pride toward his grandson, who kept his eyes on grandfather and smiled. The boy needed both hands to control his drum stick, which was as long as he was tall, his legs not long enough to reach the floor and his feet crossed at his ankles.

The grandfather then offered his drum stick to others in our group to try the rhythm, but no one did, not because we didn't want to try, but because we didn't want to break the sacredness of what we were watching. We stood in the darkened room and kept silent, just listening. We took in this precious scene unfolding before our eyes: a sacred tradition being passed through the generations. Of all the shared cultural stories and demonstrations of the day, this moment was the one that we will cherish most: seeing firsthand the baton of family history being handed to the youngest one to carry into the future.

As we left the cabin, we hiked to an area of trees nearby to pray around a prayer wheel of stones set in a circular pattern divided by a cross, looking like the dials on a compass. After our prayer, we moved just several yards to another circle of stones, this one appearing to be randomly shaped by various sizes and shapes of rocks. In the tradition of the family, each visitor chose a rock from the land and held it while praying. Walking from left to right around the pile of stones, each person placed the prayer rock onto the pile, joining it with many others who had come to pray before us.

It was impressive to see this small mound of rocks representing so many prayers from so many people. God hears our prayers and holds them to his heart forever knowing our requests, our praise, our thanks, and our desires.

One of the rocks called to me. It was triangular shaped, almost like an arrow head but not as defined. I said aloud, "I picked this one, rough around the edges, just like me." As I prayed for a concern in my family with a difficult relationship, I ran my fingers around the sharp edges of the rock, knowing that we may be hurting now, but that God has the power to smooth everything out over time. With faith that God heard my prayer, I placed my rock on the pile of prayers, walked from left to right around the circle, and felt a strong sense of faith that God has the power to restore the broken-hearted and to set us free from what holds us back from finding peace with ourselves and each other. This tangible ceremony has etched into my memory the place and time when I trusted God to use his hands to mold our family life back into a tightly knit circle of strength.

As our group prepared to leave, the grandfather raised his right hand and said with a smile, "In our culture, we do not say goodbye. We say, ("Stah - yu") meaning, "Stay strong until we meet again!"

"Stay strong." An empowering message to encourage each other. Until we meet again. A hopeful prayer for a future time when we will see each other again and share how God's strength has carried us through.

31

Spirit Reclaimed

CHAD P. SHEPHERD

I set each foot down with care, remembering childhood walks with my father. He told me of how the Native braves would learn to run silently through the forest. Long ago I learned how to slip through the woods without snapping sticks or crunching leaves. Our fellowship of nine followed our guide single file over the ancient ground.

We were an unlikely party: a Native American, a war veteran, a girl from China, an inquisitive toddler, a teenage young lady who carried the legacy of her people, a white married couple who gave without limits, a recent college graduate, and me. All of us at our own individual stage in life somehow converged in this moment to press spirit upon spirit.

We crossed under the barbed wire that marked the property line and pressed through the thorns and honeysuckle. The hillside sloped gently down underneath the cover of oak, ash, and hickory. The guide stones had led us here. This was the ancient artifact, the Shawnee prayer wheel.

Stones marked the four winds: north, south, east, and west. Smaller stones crossed the center both horizontally and vertically, forming a cross in the center. This was the traditional form of the wheel. This was used for communication with the One God, the Great Spirit. The Jews called him Yahweh. The Shawnee called him Gitche Manitou. Both identified him as the Creator of all things and the giver of life. This was a place to be purified, to confess, and to be renewed.

One's spirit could be reclaimed here.

I was in need of my spirit to experience a renewal. I considered the scope of history here, the slamming together of perspectives. Here I was, a white man descended from those who arrived on boats, being blessed by the great humility and grace of a man who was descended from those who had hunted and managed this land long before boats anchored ashore.

The present has an insistent way of slamming together with the past. Directly in the center of this Shawnee prayer wheel, verified to be from the 1700's, was a juvenile tree that grew up from its heart. It stood like a sentinel, guarding the holy site and signifying its presence.

What are we to think of this modern intrusion into the ancient divine? Should it be plucked from the earth lest its presence shift the stones and disrupt the history here? Our wise guide told us that he had long ago considered exactly that scenario. He'd not planted the tree, but he had been watching it grow for the last ten years. While he'd ripped up by the roots thousands of young trees within the proximity of the circle, this one had been something different.

It sprouted up in the perfect center. Its roots gave stability to the symmetry of the overall structure, solidifying the geometry of the pattern, preventing a shift downhill. What seemed a modern day invasion was in fact preserving the ancient ground for future generations. Joseph was recorded in Genesis 50:20 when he said from his position of power over Egypt to the very same brothers who had sold him into slavery years before, "You meant evil against me, but God used it for good."

I needed time to stop and consider this. God's ways are higher than our ways. His thoughts are bigger than our thoughts. I ponder my own life. My mistakes. My disappointments. And yet, there standing right in the middle of my mess... is God. Like a sentinel. Holding the ground, preserving the good for future generations. His presence gives order and meaning to it all.

I walked away from that place a little changed. My silent footsteps honored my dad and my renewed spirit honored my Father. May I continue to take each step with care, what the enemy of my soul meant for evil, God is using for good.

32

Campfire Magic

Nancy Hulshult

W hat is it about a campfire that calls people together to talk, to sing, to eat, and to share memorable stories under the stars? The best times are those when we sit in a circle, watch the flames sparked by kindling that heat large logs until the colors of fire rise and split into an ever-moving show of reds, oranges, even blues in the hottest spots. I can rarely take my eyes from this magical chemistry of nature.

Our family campfires were the first time that our sons were allowed to use their pocket knives, to whittle wood, to poke in the fire with hand chosen sticks, and to cook their own meals of hot dogs and s'mores. They loved to get the end of a stick red with fire and twirl it about the fire like it was a sparkler or take the end of a smoking stick and make designs in the air. They learned science lessons on their own: what would or would not burn and what it took to put the fire completely out. From their daddy, they learned how to properly use knives, how to contain the fire in the fire pit, what would explode or what would happen if the fire was left unchecked, and how to put the fire out completely before leaving the area or going to sleep.

The best part of campfires are the stories: scary stories with a startling ending, personal stories about when we were young, funny stories about our family and friends, and stories made up on the spot. My husband is the best at telling spontaneous stories. Each person picks an outlandish item to be included in the story, and Darrell finds a way to weave it into one big, surprising tale, usually of familiar characters going on an adventure into the "Enchanted Forest." This campfire tradition has made its way into our bedtime stories when the grandkids spend the night at our house.

I never thought that people actually "rolled on the ground laughing" until the night around a campfire with our kids and their friends from the youth group. Our son, Mark, had put on a rubber mask of a wrinkly-faced old man with a red hunting cap, and as is his humor, he became the old man, talking slowly, deliberately, and making up stories. We would ask him questions, and his answers made us all laugh. His improvisation and staying in character for over an hour left us breathless with laughter. That is the one and only time I saw my husband holding his stomach and rolling off his seat, a wooden log, laughing hysterically. We tried to recreate the improv at church after the youth event, and Mark was funny, but the spontaneity around the campfire still holds the record for extended laughter in our family.

The campfire has been a place of reconciliation as our youth pastor dressed like Peter and spoke to the teens about doubt, forgiveness, and being reconciled to Jesus. The campfire has been a place of testimonies where people talked about their faith in Jesus and how God has helped them to overcome life's obstacles. The campfire is a place in nature where God and humans circle up to share a moment in time. The fire reflects the light in our faces; the people reflect our thoughts in their minds; and the Holy Spirit reflects the supernatural in our hearts. And when a guitar or harmonica or acapella singing is added to the mix, well, the place turns into a heavenly sanctuary of nature!

33

Fire, Smoke, and the Winds of Change

Nancy Hulshult

They straggled in, arriving in a disjointed caravan, eager to meet again with the dozen women who regularly met in a coffee house, home, or church. With the struggles of their own and the interruptions from the pandemic, the women had been isolated from their support system, missing their monthly gatherings. Tonight their leader arrived with her usual energy and enthusiasm, bringing with her baskets of chocolate, marshmallows, and graham crackers for s'mores. She was ready with games and prizes and strategies to lift the spirits of her sisterhood, as she knew the burdens that each one carried.

When she asked me to use the retreat house and campfire for an outdoor meeting, I was happy to host and obliged to bring a devotional message. I had asked for permission for Chad to join me, and the leader respectfully took a vote of each member of the sisterhood to approve a man to present in their close knit circle. The unanimous vote relieved any reservations, and Chad and I diligently prayed and separately took the Holy Spirit's lead in choosing scripture and life applications that might resonate with the women whom we had not yet met.

My husband Darrell, Chad, and I prepared the setting for the gathering around a campfire surrounded by steady pine trees, black walnut trees ripe with green walnuts, maple trees with red and yellow leaves, and the beautiful but deadly honeysuckle with bright red berries and leafy branches.

Kindling was gathered, logs had been cut and harvested from fallen, dead trees in the deep woods. We cleared the path from the house to the fire ring of the many green walnuts that had dropped from the tall trees in the yard. We placed camping chairs, benches, and a picnic table to accommodate the dozen disciples coming to hear a word of hope and encouragement from two "inactive" pastors without church congregations. For tonight, this was our congregation, our spiritual assignment: to bring the Word of God and to make the life of Jesus mean something to this small band of believers.

My husband lit the fire and fanned the embers, and later Chad added more wood to entice the dancing flames to rise higher in their magical spectacle that captures everyone's attention under the darkened sky of an October night. Some clouds were forming with a hint of changing weather; the crescent moon outshined the scattered stars like a flashlight surrounded by a few distant candles. The tops of the trees were swaying with an autumn breeze that set the stage for a beautiful breath of fresh air of anticipation. What would the Lord have for us tonight?

From the house to the clearing, the women would have to walk down a small hill on a dirt trail with uneven gravel and occasional ruts while watching out for the baseball-sized walnuts in the grass and leaves. Several women needed assistance with our electric cart to get from their cars to their folding camping chairs. One woman walked slowly with stiff legs from sore knees in need of replacements. Another groaned quietly as she pulled herself onto the golf cart. Most walked on their own, some gingerly and others with caution, but all of them happy to see each other. Most carried foldable camping chairs and placed them in favored spots next to a friend whom they had not seen for months. Some chose chairs already in place and out of the line of smoke from the fire. The winds blew the smoke generally to one side of the fire ring, so the women rearranged their seats, some complaining of the smoke, others quietly moving, still others continuing their stories to a friend or two about their families or recent surgeries. The scene slowly morphed from an intimate circle of chairs around a fire to a linear semi-circle of fire-lighted faces in the darkness, waiting for the leader to begin.

Two huge tree stumps from the pile of firewood became the seats that Chad and I chose across from the ladies but still out of the line of smoke. We both inhaled in a bit of nervousness and anticipation before our mouths were going to speak the words that we hoped were from the Lord.

After short introductions, we spoke a word of prayer, and I began to share my admiration for the nameless Shunammite woman from 2 Kings 4 and 8. I recounted her gift of hospitality, respect for her husband, discernment to appreciate the prophet Elisha, and her strong faith that drove her daily actions. She provided a room and basic essentials specifically for Elisha's respite as he passed through town in his travels. With no expectation of pay or reward, she was happy to share her home and to befriend this holy man with the approval and permission of her husband. Elisha was moved to bless the woman and prayed that she would have her one and only son, to her great surprise and joy. While the son was working with his father in their fields, the son became ill and died. The Shunammite woman had great faith that God would bring her son back to life through the power of Elisha's prayers. Pursuing Elisha to personally return to pray over her son, the woman had laid her dead son on Elisha's bed and waited for her miracle. Indeed, God restored her son to her. After a famine that caused her to move her entire household out of Israel for seven years, she returned to ask the king to give her back her home that had been considered abandoned. The king did not know her and saw no reason to grant her request until, during a timely account of all of Elisha's miracles from his servant to the king, the king realized that this woman was the one with the resurrected son, and he restored the woman's home and all of her land and possessions to her.

As I sat on my tree stump somewhat below the level of the women's faces around the fire, I recounted the qualities of the Shunammite: hospitality, appreciation, respect, persistence, and faith. I finished with the theme of God's power of restoration. God provides, heals, and restores.

The women were silent. I had no idea how they had received my message, but I tossed the platform of the campfire to Chad, who stood and opened his bible. He shared his trepidation of having been the subject of a vote, since he had recently lost an election after tying in three run-off elections to finally lose by one vote. He said that he was happy to be speaking to a group who was unanimous in approving his presence in the circle. In the dark and facing the fire, Chad nervously shuffled his bible with his phone to light his notes. He felt impressed to lead us in a verse of "Amazing Grace." Ironically, as we sang about God's amazing grace and how "I once was lost but now am found, was blind but now I see," Chad's eyes were starting to burn and water from the smoke of the fire. I hadn't realized how long it had been since he served in a pastoral role, but I knew this ex-missionary hadn't lost his love for God and his gift for sharing scripture in relevant yet poetic ways. I knew that God would restore his vision and his calling, and this was a first step back.

As Chad opened his Bible, he opened his heart with words of wisdom about Jesus inviting his disciples into the boat: to calm them, to heal them, to guide them, and to prepare them for what was to come. Chad noted that the number of disciples in the boat huddled in close proximity to Jesus was the same as the number of people around our campfire. As he spoke, his words were accompanied by the sounds and smells of what appeared to be imminent rainfall: treetops swaying, branches bowing, and leaves waving. The smoke from the fire engulfed Chad, causing his eyes to water further, but he continued teaching. He moved a few feet to his right, but the smoke followed him.

Nevertheless, he continued breathing words of calm and healing to the women, Chad encouraged them to find the time and the space to get alone with Jesus, to huddle with disciples, and to focus on him. I didn't watch the women's reaction to Chad's words. Instead I watched what was happening with Chad. In the past week, we both had experienced a purification rite from a Native

American that involved us engulfed in the smoke of sage; both of us had written about God's restorative power through nature; and both are seeking God's purpose in unprecedented times.

From the light of the fire, I watched a second purification rite happening to Chad, only this time, he was the one moved to sing praise to God and to tell the story of our people to our people. The sage-like smoke from the fire enveloped him and calmed us, as though the Holy Spirit was physically being manifested in this smoky cloud. As his teaching came to a close, he invited us to savor the quiet, special moments with Jesus, to find the calm, to receive healing, and to listen for his direction.

In that moment, and only for a few moments, strangely the treetops quieted, the branches stopped swaying, and a different kind of delightful breeze blew through our circle. Slipping down through the clearing, and dancing past our faces, the winds seemed to cleanse our hearts from heaviness and carry them up with them toward the heavens. When Chad finished his message, he walked quietly back to his seat on the tree stump. Assignment completed. God's will be done.

None of the women spoke or responded. The leader thanked us and summarized our thoughts for the group. We prayed and then the women commenced with s'mores and some games. As I walked with Chad to his car for his return home, we could hear the laughter and chatter of the dozen left around the campfire. The mood seemed light and lively, but we weren't sure of the cause. Were they relieved that our devotions were over and they could finally open the Hershey bars and roast the marshmallows, or had God truly lifted their spirits? We both felt that we had delivered the message given to us by the Spirit, but we had no idea whether or not the women felt connected with us at all.

After Chad left, my husband helped to extinguish the fire as I helped to transport folks back up the hill to their cars. I asked the leader if everything was "alright." It was then that she shared how much the messages resonated with the women in the group, each in a different way. She

was familiar with each of their stories and said that, for many, this past year has been very difficult spiritually. Texts started to come to the leader from individual women, saying that they enjoyed the evening, loved the message (and, well, specifically "loved Chad" lol), and couldn't wait to meet again. Connection made.

It is amazing to me how God orchestrates restorative moments through nature, people, and his Word. On this night, the Lord had prompted the leader to hold a meeting around a campfire and to ask me to share a devotion. The Lord had prompted me to ask Chad and the women to agree. The Spirit had inspired Chad and me to prepare our messages independently of each other and without knowing the women's burdens or details of their stories. Having all this in place, the Lord sent his presence in the form of fire, the winds, the words, the song, the faces, and we all felt the presence of God in our midst, leaving us restored and with renewed faith in him to face another day.

After my husband and I waved goodbye to the last car pulling out of the driveway with promises to do this again soon, we stirred the embers of the flickering campfire once more. We felt light drops of rain starting to fall on our faces and held out our arms to feel the freshness of the evening rain. Looking at each other and smiling, we said, "God is good."

"All the time."

"All the time."

"God is good."

34

†ired

CHAD P. SHEPHERD

(An excerpt from my journal while leading a team of students in Central America, July 2, 2016)

The days are moving quickly and I find solace in the night. I long for solitude, isolation, and silence. I just need some time to forget myself and seek God. The voices of those who proclaim to follow God seem to never stop chattering, and the spinning of the chaos of the world has advanced to the doorstep of my heart. I cherish these days of intense fellowship with our group of ten students with Emmaus.

There is a story of Jesus' disciples, who were walking on the road from Jerusalem to Emmaus. He had been crucified, and after his death, everything they had believed was shattered. They weren't even safe any longer. They felt foolish, alone, and directionless. Suddenly, a stranger walked with them along the way. They did not recognize who he was or what he was saying, not even while he reminded them of the prophecies and promises. It wasn't until he sat with them at dinner and took the bread in his hands and broke it, giving thanks, and reached out handing it to them, that they finally realized that somehow it had been Jesus who had walked with them all evening. Their eyes were opened, they recognized him, and he disappeared from sight! They then said to each other,

"Were not our hearts burning within us while he talked with us on the road and opened the Scriptures to us?" —Luke 24:32 (NIV)

This is our goal, to encounter Jesus along the way, in the most unlikely of places. Emmaus was set up as a group of 10 college students traveling in a van driven by me, to provide them an immersive and unguarded experience of life-on-life direct experiences with the indigenous culture that has existed for thousands of years in Central America. Raw, real, unscripted. We have jobs to do, but no blueprint on how to accomplish them. Supplies are limited and our experience is null. We will travel through four countries in five weeks: Guatemala, Belize, El Salvador, and Honduras.

Our tools are shovels, pickaxes, machetes, paint brushes, Bibles, and a giant parachute with hundreds of plastic balls. We'll break our backs, share smiles and stories, and sleep under the canopy of the tropical rainforests. Howler monkeys, tarantulas, dangerous situations, and a lot of unknowns await our experience. Our little clan is bound together for the duration. No turning back, no safety net, this is survival and fellowship.

This group looks to me as their pastor and their guide. I am to be both the Shepherd of their hearts and of their corporal safety. I recognize that I feel thin, and I pray for strength, energy, and wisdom. In the quiet moonlight, while the group sleeps, I walk among them, praying, and so deeply aware that I am not qualified.

Tonight after a 15 mile drive through mountain passes, in a southwestern route out of Tikal, we are somewhere near Cobán. I can see the roof of a man known as the Chief Witch Doctor. The group that I'm leading this week is uneasy about his proximity to where we sleep in unsecured huts.

The volume of sound alone is shocking in the jungle. The insects, the inexplicable calls, howls and shrieks that compete for sound in the darkness. Our door is broken and so my bed is pressed against the open doorway. Our host gave me a machete and explained how my job is to keep the howler monkeys out of our hut. If they get in, he told me that I'd need to kill them. Of course, I laughed at his joke, and then he leaned in to my face and said, "No, this is serious."

This night was infinitely beautiful, and what in the world was I doing there with this young group of tender-footed Americans, to defend them against night terrors and what we once thought were only villains from fairy tales?

And yet... the Chief Witch... I am deeply fascinated by this man. I would love to encounter him. I imagine that I would find in him a sincere belief, maybe even more sincere than my own. I think that an intense encounter with this man could be enlightening, not because of his radically different beliefs, but because of the passion that must drive him to live out his beliefs with such commitment. I think of Elijah and the prophets of Ba'al. I think it likely that Elijah would never have been so bold to call down the fire of heaven had he not seen the futile, desperate fanaticism of the lost.

Surely I can be more committed to the one true God than the man that swirls with paint, feathers, and potions. Yet today I listened to the story of him cursing the chickens this past fall. They immediately stopped laying eggs. For three weeks, not a single egg. Then local pastors gathered and prayed over the chickens. They began laying eggs again that night. There is something real here.

There are times that I am sure that I think far too much of myself. I, too, would like to take great risks for God, but sometimes I'm not even willing to be obedient with the basics, like sharing my love for him with the people I encounter during the rush of my day.

Pastors here in Guatemala wake up and walk for miles just to meet with people that are hurting. They are going to see them, to embrace them, to cry with them, to spend the most limited commodity of time with them, and to live out the love of Christ through actions.

It's not about saving the world, how much I "just love Jesus!", or how well I can evangelize. It's about pressing into a life, touching a soul, deeply and truly loving a neighbor. Yes, I'm tired. I'm exhausted from rhetoric and sermons. I'm challenging myself to look for the man along the road, Jesus, that ate with the dirge of society, pulled water for a morally questionable woman, allowed a devoted servant to wash his feet with her hair in public, and touched the unclean.

I don't see Jesus in clean or pristine places. I see him along the rough edges of a muddy road, caked in the dirt underneath fingernails, in a shared bottle of water, and in the desperate eyes of those who know death all too well.

I see Jesus through the lives that rely on him, that bleed for him, that exist in the mud, the heat, and know that He is their comfort. The rest of us get blinded by the comforts of life and we forget that we, too, need him to survive.

I'm tired of my own heart that sometimes casually seeks him. I'm tired, and I'm going to fall back into him...for rest. I need to again throw down my own plow, and slide in beside him and allow him to pull the weight.

I want to be Paul when he was facedown on the road, Moses when he had to remove his shoes, Mary when she wept at Jesus feet and dried them with her hair, Peter when he was restored three times... I just want to stay broken.

Maybe it's just me, but I only really see him in my brokenness.

Burning the Living with the Dead

Chad P. Shepherd

There are a thousand hacking at the branches of evil to one who is striking at the root." —Henry David Thoreau

I stood on the creek bank, machete in hand. No one was here to freak out by the sight of my two-foot Colombian blade. While living in Central America, it was as common as a butter-knife, the multi-tool that could crack coconuts and split cinder blocks. I keep one in my car out of habit. Honeysuckle stood all around me and blocked my progress. I began to swing, dropping branches with a slash. As they fell, more and more branches seemed to crowd me. The absence of one branch seemed to set loose the previously bound tension of another. A branch hit me in the face and slapped my sunglasses to an apparent abyss. They were never found.

The more I hacked, the more the vines seemed to take on life of their own, crowding in thicker and deeper, growing more robust and harder to cut. I began to sweat and had to stop to catch my breath. In the solace of that cease-fire, a slow smile crept across my branch-slapped face. Only a couple of feet away from me, on the slope of the creekbank, stood the root of the tree that plagued me. I already saw the end of the battle. I reached down for the bottle of water that had fallen from my pocket in the fray. The cool water refreshed my throat. I gripped the machete in my right hand and began to swing. The arc of the blade hissed through the air and landed a satisfying "thunk" into the root. I swung and I swung and I swung until that hand-sharpened blade laid waste to the target. The tree was decapitated from its root and crumpled down the bank into the water.

Sweat dripped from my chin. I could now feel the breeze that came from the canopy above. I stood in the silence until I was again joined by the sounds of the birds. I stood longer, and I heard the chatter of a squirrel. The interloper had been removed. Now the indigenous foliage of the land would be free to bloom in the sunlight. A thousand hacks at the branches could not yield the result of a mere dozen swings at the root. It was never about the effort; it was about the focus.

I've lost focus in my life. I've hacked and swung and sweated and spun until I was breathless to find nothing but destruction and exhaustion. These are the times that I've lost focus. These are the times that have resulted in loss. Sometimes at no fault of my own, and sometimes pride and stubbornness, would keep me swinging in vain. I would do well to remember my identity.

"I am the vine and my Father is the vine grower. He removes every branch in me that bears no fruit... Whoever does not abide in me is thrown away like a branch and withers; such branches are gathered, thrown into the fire, and burned. His winnowing fork is in his hand, and He will clear his threshing floor, and gather his wheat into the granary, but the chaff He will burn with unquenchable fire," (my paraphrase from John 15:1-7, Luke 3:17, NRSV/NIV).

The background noise of my childhood was the dread of my adolescence, the desperate attempt of redemption for a young man, and finally, the unexpected identity of this veteran soul. Constant and steady truth met with never-ending shifts in my personal perspective. What was once noise is now the symphony that pushes back my insanity. I calm my soul and listen to the crack and pop of the burning branches. My life is like a blended vineyard, of some branches that grew beautiful fruit, and others that just shriveled with death and became dust on the ground. Together they burn... what is alive and what is dead.

I am gripped by this realization. My own soul burns with what was once alive and with what needs to die. I am this inferno of past and present, of angel and demon. It all burns together. This is the only way of purification. The dry and dead fuels and heats the green and living. The stuff of the past and branches of the present. It all must burn together to be refined. The smoke causes my eyes to tear and I watch little wisps of what once was floating away on the evening breeze. What remains after the refining fire of God is all that is good.

There have been times that I've stood on the creek bank of my life, exhausted, forced to stillness, only to realize that my pursuits had been selfish. Marriage lost. Promises broken. Trusts betrayed. Silence and darkness crushing in and slashing at my face, knocking off my sight and obscuring my vision somehow into the abyss.

I think of King David.

"Generous in love—God, give grace!
Huge in mercy—wipe out my bad record.
Scrub away my guilt, soak out my sins in your laundry.
I know how bad I've been;my sins are staring me down."
—Psalms 51:1-3 (MSG)

Yes, that's it. I felt so dirty in those moments, like there was no going back. The stink is too thick; it's like stepping in dog poop with your favorite shoes. You pick up a stick and try to carve the foulness out of the treads from your nasty situation while gagging from the smell that saturates your mouth. Blech!

"You're the One I've violated, and you've seen
it all, seen the full extent of my evil.
You have all the facts before you;
whatever you decide about me is fair.
I've been out of step with you for a long time,
in the wrong since before I was born.
What you're after is truth from the inside out.
Enter me, then; conceive a new, true life."
—Psalms 51:4-6 (MSG)

Back in the fall of 1998, I lived in Monroe, Ohio, just behind the high school football field. I had a golden retriever named Zach, and

I loved to take him on late night walks. One night he and I were crossing the field at midnight when we spotted a cat, center field. We were on the 30 yard line when Zach began to bark at that cat. The cat suddenly turned and ran towards the woodline. Zach bolted and the leash slipped from my hand! Suddenly, a cat, a dog, and a human began a wild dash that rivaled any Friday night lights chase on that field. I am confident, also, that never in the history of Monroe High School football has a chase ever ended so violently, and so abruptly.

Without warning, the cat stopped running and did a headstand, front legs on the field and rear end in the air. Did you know that skunks make a sound when they shoot their spray? I did not hold that knowledge until that moment. That was no cat! Zach the dog took the hit directly in the eyes. I also learned that night that dogs can scream. I was wearing shorts and the skunk-shot hit me in the kneecaps. The potency of the offense was shocking. It stung my skin and shot up my nose, causing me to throw up a little in my mouth.

I remember the look on my wife's face when I burst through the door butt-naked, having discarded my clothes in the garage, and streaked through the house directly to the shower. As I ran past her with tears in my eyes, I heard her gag as the smell hit her.

Like King David, I have had times when my own actions were so vile to me that I felt as though even the dogs were screaming from the stench of my sins, and everyone just saw me running naked in my shame. The people that I was supposed to love and protect were gagging at my actions. I found myself desperately crying out to God to cleanse me.

> **"Soak me in your laundry and I'll come out clean,**
> **scrub me and I'll have a snow-white life.**
> **Tune me in to foot-tapping songs,**
> **set these once broken bones to dancing.**

Don't look too close for blemishes,
give me a clean bill of health.
God, make a fresh start in me,
shape a Genesis week from the chaos of my life."
—Psalms 51:7-10 (MSG)

Another thing I learned that fateful and odoriferous night, tomato juice absolutely does not remove the stench of skunk spray. I soaked in the bathtub for an hour, shivering in gallons of tomato juice. It was a minor version of Hell, I looked like Carrie at the high school prom. It was humiliating and mortifying. Sin is exactly like that. No matter how long I sat there, the stench did not dissipate.

We turned to the internet and found that there was a solution: one part Dawn dish detergent, one part vinegar, and one part baking soda. The article explained that the skunk spray is an ingenious and evil invention of nature. It is an oil. That oil, when it hits you, sinks into the pores on your skin. The only way to remove the smell is to remove the oil. That made sense and I was eager to proceed.

My learning experience that night continued. What the article failed to tell me was that the solution produced a chemical reaction that resulted in a mild burn to my skin. It said to apply the solution with a brush, which I did. It hurt, but at least my swollen and pink legs were thankfully odor free.

Sometimes cleansing hurts, especially when we need a deep cleaning. It's no different with God. Sometimes the "Genesis week" that we require means that the chaos of the darkness has to be split by the searing fire and light of God separating the night from the day. However, that moment when we're finally clean makes it worth the pain.

"Don't throw me out with the trash,
or fail to breathe holiness in me.
Bring me back from gray exile,

put a fresh wind in my sails!
Give me a job teaching rebels your ways
so the lost can find their way home.
Commute my death sentence, God, my salvation God,
and I'll sing anthems to your life-giving ways.
Unbutton my lips, dear God;
I'll let loose with your praise."
—Psalms 51:11-15 (MSG)

This is now my prayer, my life, my focus. God did not leave me like a heap of skunk-sprayed clothes in the garage. He did not bag me and put me in the rubbish bin. He cleansed me completely, and in the burning process, he helped me to remember my identity, my purpose, and my calling. The skunked can be scoured, the dirtiest can be cleaned, and the lost can find their way back home.

For this reason I fall on my knees at my bedside every night, and I give big praise to my God. He has unbuttoned my lips, and he has cleansed the stench from my flesh. My life is an anthem to him because I know that I deserved the stench of death that covered me, but he is the one who cleansed me.

I accepted the grace that he offers to all sinners, and it shattered me in all of the best of ways. God's promises are true. He will never leave us. We can never be too far from him. "If we confess our sins, he is faithful and just to forgive us our sins and to cleanse us from all unrighteousness," (1 John 1:9 ESV). He created us and he is always reaching out to us. His love is real, and it is never too late to come back home.

While I was hacking away at the branches of that honeysuckle, God waited for me to find my way to the root cause of my sin. Sometimes in life we allow pride or our own agendas to branch out into a thousand branches of confusion that cloud our judgment or even block our way. Even in those moments, if we pause to listen and calm our frenzied pursuits, God calls us to refocus us back to the root of what needs to be cleansed from our lives.

Sometimes the land must be purified through labor, death, and fire. I stand in the smoke and consider this against my own journey. I've been through a time of purification. It required hard work on my own part: self-examination, honesty, and change. It required death from bad habits and dangerous thinking. It required the hot fire of regret, grief, and even despair. Purification and reclamation come only with a price.

We must work for it. We must accept death to the old self. We must be willing to have our past and our present to be purified by fire. Only then are we again prepared for the new life of our indigenous soul to rise from the ash. We must work for it, and yet we also must freely accept it. The highest price was paid by that master vine grower. Who I am is forever found in him.

36

Undesirable Species

Nancy Hulshult

W hat do I know? After 60 years on this beautiful yet deadly earth, I don't know a whole lot about anything. My truths are simple. Jesus saves, Heaven is eternal, and this world and everything in it is temporary...all of it, the humans, the wildlife, the seashores, and, really, our whole planet. Yes, time flies and we need to take time to stop and smell the flowers.

Recently, I did just that. I skipped church on a Sunday morning and listened to an online sermon while I walked the grounds of the retreat center that my husband and I maintain for people to come and rest and recharge, to get close to nature and to God. As I listened to the pastor's message about the organic church made up of contagious Christians who love and serve God everywhere, inside and outside of church walls, I walked slowly through the first few acres of our natural preserve. I took notice of the colorful flowers embedded in the grass and the woods and began to take close-up photos of each one. Then my eye caught an old wooden gate, a mud-covered bridge, a big boulder, and an abandoned birdhouse nailed to a tree.

After hearing the sermon and closing worship music, I returned to the house, took a few notes, and posted my appreciation of the pastor's message for us to take action instead of limiting ourselves to sitting in pews and serving each other. I was so inspired that I posted my photos of nature's beauty and wrote: "Walking in nature, listening to pastor's sermon, and thanking God for every blessed thing that He has created for his and our enjoyment. ..come and see...with grateful hearts...."

I awoke this morning with a revelation. I was thinking of the posted photos of the things that nobody wanted or that everyone had abandoned. The undesirable was desirable and lovely to me: the red honeysuckle berries highlighted by the green leaves, the wild purple violets, the white clover, the yellow sweetclover, and the white bursts of gentweed blossoms. All of these weeds, if not put in check, can take over a garden, lawn, or woods and would be killed by gardeners and lawn owners. Most people would repair the broken gate, clear the muddy bridge, let the boulder sit there doing nothing, and replace the old, abandoned birdhouse for one that attracted more birds.

Yet I noticed each undesirable thing and enjoyed the beauty of each, even shared a picture of each with the world. I asked the world to come and see and thank God for every blessed thing created for his and our enjoyment.

What must they think of my values and knowledge of nature (or lack thereof)? I had to chuckle at my apparent love of weeds, broken, muddy, and abandoned things, and rocks that don't do anything. In my reflective time today, I realize that this really does say a lot about me and who I am as a person. I guess that I don't always see life as others do, and my approach to ministry life leads me to see people in a different light, to see people as God sees them. Those who some may consider to be invasive, broken, dirty, and abandoned, I seem to notice and enjoy the beauty in their resiliency, their ability to survive in the most dire circumstances, their desire to get healthier, even through their circumstances that would predict otherwise.

I believe my heart has been transformed by the cross-cultural experiences on mission workcamps and in urban schools. I believe that my world view has changed over the years. In my mind's eye, I still see the sparkle in the eyes of a hungry child taking the rest of his school food home to his siblings. I still hear the joyful sound of underserved kids in an urban schoolyard with broken fences and cracked concrete. I still smell the tortillas baking on a stone in an outdoor kitchen of a tented barrio. I still taste the sour milk scent on the breath of an abandoned baby in an orphanage. I still enjoy the visits of the wanderer in the aluminum foil hat. I still learn from the brilliant college professor living in the homeless shelter in the Bronx. I still delight in giving an extra scoop of beans to the woman with the toothless smile. I still raise my voice in a worship to a song sung by an unchurched transvestite. I still feel the warmth from the freshly laundered clothes for the lice-ridden school girl.

I suppose that "undesirable" people, the poor and the oppressed, are like undesirable plants. They can survive where others of their species won't, but their situations can be overwhelming unless kept in check. And truly, the people are not undesirable. Poverty and violence is. Unless we do something to prevent poverty and oppression, it will invade our species as human beings and as children of God. There are only so many places where we can hide our ghettos, run off our homeless from under our bridges, lock up our addicts, and turn a deaf ear to our victims of violence and abuse. If our lack of noticing and valuing each person goes unchecked, then all of our species will be at risk of becoming inhumane.

I cannot just ask the world simply to take notice. I want to take action, to do more to help. I want to be a contagious Christian who helps to spread the Gospel of Jesus Christ, to do what we have been commanded to do.

> *Love the Lord your God with all your heart and with all your soul and with all your mind and with all your strength. The second is this: 'Love your neighbor as yourself.' There is no commandment greater than these."* —Mark 12:30-31 (NIV)

37

Sterling Mei Dances in the Moonlight

Chad P. Shepherd

March 5, 2012, Guangzhou, China

She danced above the water and below the stars, held in my arms. The neon skyline of Guangzhou passed us by as periphery while our eyes were locked on each other. Kellie and I took turns spinning her as we moved to the sound of the music. The breeze off the top of the river was warm and the entire dance floor was ours. My daughter in my arms, and my wife embracing us both. I found love all over again.

The Chinese passengers of the river-cruise boat sipped their tea and watched as the American couple disregarded their presence and pretended that the moment could last forever. Kellie and I smiled and laughed as the music turned from classical to Spanish, and we found that we knew the song.

As we moved across the top of the ship, with my daughter smiling and laughing those incredible baby laughs in my ear, I realized that she would never remember this night. She would have no recollection of sharing her first ever dance with her father and mother in the land of her birth, on the day we celebrate her path to American citizenship.

She wore a pink dress with white printed tights and leather slippers with flowers embroidered on the toes. She held her hands up in the air as she leaned her head back, looking at the sky as we spun. She would peek up to see if I was watching her. When we stopped, she would bob her head from side to side and clap her hands, until we began again. The nanny that cared for her told us that this girl was "crazy and dangerous." Indeed, we stood there amazed at how perfectly she fits into the way we tackle life.

For over an hour we danced across that ship top, reflecting on an incredible past several days. It really seems impossible that we have only held her in our arms for only about a week. She already has been with us forever. I can't imagine what our life was like without her. She may only be 14 months old, but she has been in our hearts for nearly six years. It is fulfilling beyond measure to hold her in the moonlight.

There were other adoptive families on board as well, but they did not join in. I am sure some of them will go home and tell of the crazy couple that spun about the third deck of a moving boat in the nighttime air with their infant daughter, probably with some disdain in their voice, but I wish they could have experienced what translated into pure magic for our family on this incredible night.

Sometimes you've got to live life by being a bit eccentric. Sometimes you just need to recognize the incredible wonder in the moment. Sterling may not remember this night, but we have photos, and you can be sure that we will tell her about how we danced with her tear-sparkled smiles on our faces in the warm moonlight.

I know there will be more dances in her future: dances where I am sitting up at night awaiting her return; and a dance where she is wearing white, and I will once again get to spin her on the floor while others watch, while the two of us share a magic moment, as if no one were watching. On that day for sure, I know what I will be whispering in her ear.

I will tell her of this night, and how her mother and I shared her very first dance. I will tell her never to miss an opportunity to show the world how much you enjoy the ones you love.

She may not remember, but we will never let her forget.

38

WALKING WITH DRAGONS

CHAD P. SHEPHERD

The air is perfect tonight. It is late September and a little bit of warm air has returned to let us know that mother nature is not quite ready to yet give up the summer. The autumn equinox may have passed, but summer has an encore! Tomorrow is forecasted to be a warm 84 degrees and I plan to warm my skin in its beam. For tonight, it is a perfectly wonderful landscape to walk with my dog in the glow of the lights of the night, wearing running shoes, cut-off jeans, a simple t-shirt, and my favorite black jacket.

The sign near the water of the pond reads, "No swimming, boating, rafting, or skating." It is cleverly disguised to look like a classic wooden post and planks, but it is a prefab steel replica of what was once substance. It lacks the pull and wear that accompanies true world time and space. Ironically, it presents as artificial nostalgia, poorly cloaked in this modern world mimicry of things that once held value.

Conversely, the night sounds are abundant and unmistakably refreshing. Crickets are the big deal, their sounds reminding me of my childhood reading of A Cricket in Times Square, and a fascination of that micro-universe within that self-inflated city. I was so captivated by that book. One little cricket in the glare and movement of that giant city! We all possess so much magic, the stuff of potential that outshines the challenges of living. There are things in this life that yet remind me of that.

I look at my 10-year-old daughter. She has not yet abandoned the magic. She fears bees and wrestles with the conundrum of whether wolves or dragons are the coolest of creatures. Today she and I agreed that a wolf-dragon would be the ultimate of creatures. I mean, why not? The Never Ending Story had a "Luck Dragon" that was a combination of a dog and a dragon. Surely a combination of a wolf and a dragon would be an upgrade.

Author Michael Ende, what do you say? I'm thinking that Sterling is onto something, and you and my daughter could collaborate to add to your "Luck Dragon" concept to create the "Wolf Dragon." It would be the natural progression of the story. Wolves are instinctually pack animals. They are intuitive, typically not aggressive, intelligent, and get unreasonable negative press sometimes. This girl of mine, she causes me, a Shepherd, to romanticize the wolf.

I bought her dragon earrings today. They were the pure dragon, non-wolf type. They looked amazing with her dark hair. The smile on her face was confirmation of their absolute perfection. We had looked at them earlier online, combing through thousands of designs. The earrings that seized her attention and animated her choice were remarkably similar to the tattoo of a dragon on my left shoulder that is the tattoo symbolizing her: my Chinese little fierce fire-breather.

I had that tattoo made while we were awaiting her adoption. China had just shut down adoptions to the U.S. We had the choice of switching to another country or waiting on the chance that adoptions might re-open. I doubled down with a permanent skin commitment, and after six years, Sterling came home.

In this world of fear, of rules, of masks that cover our faces, tonight was a simple walk under the stars with my dog by my side. I pull the air into my lungs, and I taste the night. It tastes exactly like the nights of my childhood in Preble County, Ohio. It tastes like that night in Guangzhou when I spun in the moonlight over the Yellow River, holding my little daughter in my arms on a midnight cruise.

There is magic yet to be held in this world. You don't need a Luck Dragon or even a Wolf Dragon. I pause to really listen to the sound of the simple cricket. I stop to open the eyes of my heart and look at the people who matter to me most. I take this moment to think of the best memories of my life and pull from those snapshots the bits of wonder that made me. Now I make this declaration: this is who I am, and who you are, created to be.

Created with a unique purpose for this time, we are our fears, our risks, our experiences, hopes and dreams. Oh, how remarkable it is when I consider that no one else on this planet is quite the equation of me, or of Sterling. Don't go softly into this night.... open your eyes to the dragons and wolves and the 10-year-old visions of this world.

There is beauty and adventure, even meaning and peace, yet here to be found. It is time to swim, to raft, to boat, and to skate. The sign is nothing more than a distraction.

39

When She Asked the Question

Chad P. Shepherd

November 20, 2015

Aleks is growing up and I found myself slowing down enough to see her this week. I'm glad that I took the time. There is wisdom and a soft kindness in her eyes. I'm not one of those types that regret the passage of time, and watching my children grow is by far the most enjoyable part of my life. I love seeing them become.

"Dad, if you could be anywhere in the entire world right now, doing anything you wanted to do, where would you be?"

We were floating together in a small saltwater pool on the southern Pacific coast of Guatemala, on a strip of land that becomes an island when the tide crashes in. A river ran behind the small open air beach house, and the moon was rising full with its glow reflecting on her face from the water.

We began the day with sunlight sparkling on the black sand, bacon and eggs, surrounded by my mom and dad and a couple of close friends. After breakfast, I spent four hours writing on the topic of the forgiven woman who washed Jesus' feet with her tears and wiped them with her hair.

We'd spent the day isolated from the chaos of the world, no a/c, no phones, no televisions, limited power, and a jug of water for drinking. Christmas music played softly on a blue-tooth speaker, and card games replaced technology.

Dinner was shared family style around a crowded table with seconds for all and more than we needed. Even Remus, the family dog, seemed to drink deeply from the warmth of the day.

I pondered her question and considered the places I'd like to see: the history and wonder of Israel, Big Ben in England, the barrier reef in Australia, the Grand Canyon, diving on the ocean floor into untouched ruins, or maybe orbiting the moon that highlighted her smiling, wide-eyed face.

I let the moonlight shape a smile on my face as I yielded to the obvious. "Here. Right now. I think today has been a perfect kind of day." I was afraid that she might challenge my answer because she knows my wandering heart. She didn't though. She considered it and nodded.

I saw her this week. I saw the perspective of my life from this new place. I give thanks this Thanksgiving holiday from the depths of my soul. It streams from some deep place in my core. I am thankful.

I knew this... when she asked the question.

40

Time To Let You Go....Fly!

CHAD P. SHEPHERD

August, 2021

The sunlight at the pool today has a monochromatic lens, its beams too intense and technicolor for my hypoxic heart. The memories of our beginning boomerang around my delirious mind. The nannies called you, "Zaichik," the little bunny. You are my Zaichik, my only sunshine, my Sasha. I remember the day your infant face turned, and our eyes collided in that stark fluorescent Soviet block building. I knew in that moment that you were mine.

I remember the Russian official at her heavy wooden desk with her formal uniform as she looked me sternly in the eye and asked me a series of questions: "Do you promise to love her? Do you promise to never abandon her? Do you promise to never abuse her? Do you understand that she now will always be yours?"

Yes, she has always been mine: my Goldilocks, my ballerina, my one day cheerleader, my gymnast, my Brownie, my Sunday School volunteer, my running partner, swimming partner, popcorn sharer, Halloween dress-up partner, driving student, homework buddy, and travel buddy. We've been inseparable for nearly 18 years.

Only today do I understand why I have felt so devastated and wrecked. You are no longer mine. You are now your own. I mean, I guess really you always have been your own, but now I realize that you're no longer the little bunny safe in my arms. You are beyond the institution, beyond your childhood, and beyond my myopic gaze.

This is obvious and somehow shocking to me. How is it that my Zaichik has grown wings?

It is natural really. She has always been the most intensive, independent, fierce soul that I've ever known. Haha, I remember when she was a toddler, I was trying to give her just half a stick of chewing gum. Her immediate response was that little hand waving in my face as she said, "No piece! No piece!" There was no peace as long as she did not get fully included into everything!

She was the little girl who wanted to be at my side constantly. I remember making her go and play alone in her room for 20 minutes by herself so that I could get some work done. She cried. Now it is me crying as she has found her own room at a university miles away.

I've never before in my life wanted to return to a moment, yet I'd throw away everything I have to return to that moment when I first held her in my arms, just so I could relive it all again, and this time savor it more.

I began writing these words the evening after driving away without her. I understand now, so fully, the tears of my parents when they drove away. I was off to the adventure of my life, but they felt abandoned. One day, she'll also get the other side of this perspective, and I'll be beside her sobbing as we together watch the next generation take flight.

I will confess that I had to stop writing this ten days ago. My words kept descending into despair. I knew it was ridiculous. I knew she was exactly where she was meant to be, where she'd always said she'd be, where I always hoped she'd be: taking that first solo flight. Still I felt so desperately alone. I'd tell myself that cognitively I knew I was being unreasonable. Then a coworker would ask me about her, and I'd openly sob in front of any and every person who was present. I was useless for days. I didn't care who saw me weep.

They say that you can run out of tears. That is a lie.

Then she video called me one evening, and I saw her face. I'd never seen that particular smile before. I mean, I've seen a lot of different smiles on her face, but never one quite like that. It was the smile of a raven who had had her entire perspective reshaped after that first flight into the open sky.

So here again I sit at the pool. The deep emerald water, surrounding green trees, and golden sunlight on my skin all prove to me that the color has returned to my world. Yes, it is time to let her go, and I'm working on that. It is going to take some time.

But unlike a few days ago, I wouldn't go back, and I wouldn't change a thing. She's landed perfectly where she is created to be.

So you go, girl, go! I love you, and my promises remain. I'll always love you, never abandon you, and while you'll always be mine, I understand now that I never really held you. You are held in a higher purpose by the One who holds us both. And now you soar on wings like eagles, like Ravens!

It is as it should be, because your pursuit gets all of you. To any who would try to limit you, just hold up that sweet, fierce hand, and proclaim, "No piece! No piece!"

Take it all.

41

I Don't Know What I'd Do Without You

CHAD P. SHEPHERD

"It's just me and you now, kiddo." This is our new reality and it is like I'm just now waking up. There have been too many incomprehensible events in my life over the last six months.

Caleb graduated from Cedarville University and then moved to Minnesota for the summer. Aleks graduated from Carmel High School and then left to be on campus at Anderson University. And Sterling, she has grown up so much this summer. I'm getting glimpses already of the young lady she will become, and I'm all too aware of how quickly her next seven years are going to pass.

I am so thankful for her. She was the third one to call me "Dad," and now she is the only one left that still sees me with childhood eyes, but oh my, how that is already changing.

I've really gotten to know her this summer. She and I took a road trip to see my parents at Myrtle Beach, 14 hours each way, conversations and Taylor Swift. McDonald's and holding our breath through the tunnels were great memories with a six foot stuffed unicorn riding shotgun.

Today she sat with me poolside. After four hours she was clearly bored out of her mind, and the arrival of two sisters, one a high school senior and the other a college student, pushed the both of us over the edge. They spoke like California valley girls and their voices were shrill and loud. We packed up our towels and sunscreen, rapidly making our exit.

This evening was about capturing the day. It was time to make memories with this one. I drove her to the local theater and bought two tickets to see Disney's Jungle Cruise with Dwayne Johnson. It was surprisingly good, reminding me of when my uncle Stephen took me to see Indiana Jones and the Temple of Doom when I was about Sterling's age. The universe felt good and full circle today.

After a dinner at Texas Roadhouse (gotta love those rolls), we returned to the apartment and took a late-night stroll with Dinah the dog. Sterling asked if we'd be safe. I showed her the .45 concealed on my hip. She asked me if I'd show her some self-defense moves, so we worked on how to defend and escape an attacker. She nearly broke my foot!

Afterwards we watched Hotel Transylvania, and I was stunned how the relationship between Dracula and his daughter mirrored BOTH how I recently had to release Aleks and these tender days that I still have with Sterling. I am so filled with emotion. I am so thankful.

I'm fighting my way back into a good place. God has been faithful to me, far more than I deserve. As we were winding the night down, Sterling walked up to me and said, "Dad, I don't know what I'd do without you."

She had my full attention and my whole heart. Our eyes held a steady exchange as smiles broke over both of our faces. Finally I responded, "Sterling, I think I'd be pretty messed up without you."

This day has been such a wonderful experience. This is life. While I still sting from the transition of my two older children, I recognize the magic of this young life that still is under my roof. I am a blessed man. The two big kids are doing what they've been raised to do, but I am not yet done with Unicorn Dreams and Jungle Cruises.

42

Are We There Yet?

Chad P. Shepherd

The sound of the fountains below my fourth floor apartment provide the music of the night. The new fresh air of these fall nights pulse into my window with a rhythm nearly like breathing. This is the time of day when the busyness yields to the quiet. My body rests as my soul reviews the day and reasserts itself as the ruler of my heart.

My mind has so much to process of the day. I think of my three children, and I picture them safe and sound. I shove worry out of my head and instead paint for them sweet dreams as I talk to God about their future. My mind wanders to a lady whom I've known for some time, and I pray fervently that perhaps her affections might again turn my way.

The night for me holds hope. The depth of the cosmos on display, lighting up eternity. I can literally see for years, for light years. My eyes take hold of things that once were, are now, and are yet to come. The surface tension of my soul is no less greater than that of the sun, and the resulting revolutions of its gravity pulls all that I love closer to me.

Liminal space. That is exactly where I find myself on this early autumn night. Liminal space, the physical space between one destination and the next, a cosmic way station. A Latin rooted word that describes this time between what was and what's next.

"Are we there yet, Daddy?"

The liminal space of a road trip. Are we there yet? And what do we do in the intermittent time? We remember who we are, celebrating stories and memories. We are present in the moment, playing license plate games and seeing who can hold their breath through the mountain tunnels. We talk about our preferred future and we plan our days. We remember that we are in this together. Liminal space... what seems merely transitory, is in fact... definitive.

There is no wasted time on this planet. The in between moments prepare us for our next. The sound of the fountains, the feel of the breeze, the smell of the cool autumn air... it all stills our heart for what is yet to come. This is the still, small voice of God.

She had my full attention and my whole heart. Our eyes held a steady exchange as smiles broke over both of our faces. Finally I responded, "Sterling, I think I'd be pretty messed up without you."

43

He Hated My Earrings

Chad P. Shepherd

"Hi Pop. Are you going to talk to me tonight? It has been a while since you've visited. I miss you and I could really use your conversation."

"Pop" is what I called my maternal grandpa. My mother's dad. His name was Carmel, but to me he is forever "Pop." I never even thought of it as an aberrant referral to grandpa, it was simply who he was. The whole family called him "Pop."

Family lore said that he was "Pop" because at a Christmas gathering, his growing stomach placed too much pressure on his shirt and the button "popped off." According to family lore, that was the origin of his name... but I'm not sure... I think I knew him as "Pop" long before that episode. I think it just cemented the moniker. Probably, Pop was just what his kids (my mom and her siblings) called him as they grew up. Even so... I love the button-pop story and well, how about we just go with it?

He died. It was a shock to me. He'd been dying for years, but still the moment of his passing just seemed far too abrupt. I mean... he was living and breathing. And then he was just... dead.

No.

I had never had a moment of life without Pop.

His voice had always been strong. His eye contact, intense. His words... unfiltered. One thing that he had NEVER been... was silent. The silence was unbearable. It was so evident of his absence.

I remember when we met for dinner at Olive Garden. It was the first time he saw my earrings. He had tears in

Me & Pop

his eyes and I've never felt so awful. I was making my grandpa cry.

He asked, "Buck (he called all of his sons and me Buck... I have no idea why) are you still my good little Chad?" I answered "Yes." I'll confess now, though, that I was not. As he feared, my physical appearance was representative of the condition of my heart. But what was I to say in that moment? I did not want to cause a scene at a family gathering. "Pop, you know I am. I love you." He nodded and hugged me so tight. So tight.

When I was unfaithful to my marriage so long ago... he came to me. Weeping. Filling my heart with truths. I am so thankful. He saved me then. I returned to my wife and we spent an additional decade raising our children. Thank you, Pop. You gave us that.

Here is what I cannot explain. I still talk to him, he visits me while I sleep. The setting is sometimes the living room of his and Mamaw's house on Marcie drive, sometimes it is at my uncle Stephen's house where he lived and died... and sometimes he literally stands at the foot of my bed and speaks to me and in those moments I feel awake and present.

He still scowls at my earrings. And he tells me that he loves me. He asks me how I am doing. He listens to me and he smiles at me. He tells me how much he loves Caleb, Aleks, and Sterling. He tells me that they are special and he asks me if I realize how blessed I am. He weeps when I speak of my divorce, and he speaks encouragement when I mention my future.

He mourns my losses, celebrates my blessings, and gives me hope for the future. He is my Pop.

I miss his toothpick that he chewed on, his hat that always perched sideways on his head. His scent of Old Spice and wing-tip shoes. I miss his arm that would be around my shoulders on Sunday night prayer meetings. He was my Pop, and he made my world feel safe.

And here I am now.

My earrings have grown from two to six. I am no longer married. My household is split. I am at the mercy of a crucified God. And I find mercy. I talk to my Pop at night. I swear it is really him. He isn't happy about every decision that I've made... and yet, he is still my Pop. His love shines through his eyes and he sees that I'm doing my best with what I have in this moment. He continues to give me unconditional love, like the Father's love.

That is his ring. He wore it for years. It is 10 carat gold and I don't know if the stone is diamond or composite. Frankly I don't care. The worth of this ring far exceeds its composition. This ring was on the hand of the man who wrapped his arms around me for so many years... and even now... finds a way to talk to me in my dreams.

Pop. I'm trying here. I love you. I know I've made some pretty major mistakes. But I also know that this story isn't yet over. The God you taught me to love, He is still with me. I cannot escape him. Your influence still covers me. Your ring sets on my finger.

I look at it daily. Every single day. I see it as your legacy and God's promise. My story is not yet fully written. Your ring, your legacy, your promise to God... it yet lives on in me.

Broken and imperfect. Even earring bearing... and yet the Love of God and you... compel me. Let's do some crazy Kingdom things... earrings and imperfections and all.

God uses broken vessels. I am a broken vessel. I am used by God.

2 Timothy 2:15 (ESV) says: "Do your best to present yourself to God as one approved, a worker who does not need to be ashamed and who correctly handles the word of truth."

Amen.

44

Dirt and Spit

NANCY HULSHULT

Masks. Fist bumps. Hand sanitizers. Social distancing. Even isolation. Living in a pandemic keeps us so far from one another because we don't want to catch a virus, get deathly sick, and die on a ventilator. I read the Bible about Jesus' miracles and see how close Jesus was to people, not just the crowds who wanted to hear him teach Truth, but also those who needed physical healing. He spat on the ground and anointed a man's eyes with a mix of mud and his saliva, then told him to wash in the Pool of Siloam (John 9:1-12). Jesus put his fingers into a man's ears, then spit and touched the man's tongue. Eww! (Mark 7:33) He spit on a man's eyes and put his hands on a blind man. (John 9:6) Why did people allow Jesus to put his hands on them, to spit on them, to stick his fingers into their ears? Why did the lepers bathe in the river at his command and get healed of their leprosy? Because they had faith and did what it took for them to be healed. Not only did Jesus show that he was a healer, he also demonstrated his power over nature, demons, life and death.

Jesus restored people using elements of nature, and he showed his deity by demonstrating power over nature. Jesus calmed the storms, walked on water, was transfigured with the supernatural on a mountain, fed multitudes with a little bread and a few fish; he cursed a fig tree to make it wither; and he was in constant communication with God the Father through prayer. Jesus was in his natural and supernatural element on earth where he walked and taught, on the cross where he died, in the ground where he was buried, and in the skies when he was resurrected and returned to heaven. Jesus, as God made man, flowed effortlessly in both the natural and supernal realms, and he still does today. By the power and the authority of Jesus, we pray in his name to heal people and to restore souls today.

God created us, his image bearers, by using the dust of the earth. (Genesis 2:7) He blew his own supernatural breath into our nostrils to bring us life. God uses the natural by forming us from dirt and then the supernatural by breathing his life into us. The dirty, earthy part of our being caused us to spit in God's face by misusing his laws that governed the Garden. We ate forbidden fruit in an effort to become supernatural like God. We were cursed for our sin and made to work the ground for our food.

Even in our state of sin, God demonstrates his restorative power through nature. Through the study of biology and the other sciences of nature, we have learned of healing elements of certain plants that can cure some diseases and help us to live healthier lives. However, God's plan goes beyond a better life in the natural world. He had a supernatural plan to reunite us with him for eternity.

To lift our eyes from working the ground to the face of God, He sent his Son Jesus through the purest earthly form of human vessel, Mary, to show people how to live, how to love, and how to be saved from death to eternal life with God. God loves all that He created and uses creation to teach, to heal, and to bring us back into unity with him.

John describes the Garden of Eden restored as the leaves of the tree of life bring healing to the people.

> *Then the angel showed me the river of the water of life, as clear as crystal, flowing from the throne of God and of the Lamb down the middle of the great street of the city. On each side of the river stood the tree of life, bearing twelve crops of fruit, yielding its fruit every month. And the leaves of the tree are for the healing of the nations. No longer will there be any curse. The throne of God and of the Lamb will be in the city, and his servants will serve him. They will see his face, and his name will be on their foreheads. There will be no more night. They will not need the light of a lamp or the light of the sun, for the Lord God will give them light. And they will reign for ever and ever.*
> —(Revelation 22:1-5 NIV)

We may not feel comfortable taking off our masks and getting closer to humans in the spatio-temporal dynamics of a pandemic, but we can make an effort to get closer to Jesus in this time of spiritual renewal and hope of eternal life with God. In a quiet sanctuary of nature, away from the crowds, we may find God's restorative power: to find calm in our storms, food for our souls, faith in our walk, balance in our emotions, clearer vision of ourselves and others, and an intimate connection with the supernatural in the natural.

45

Spit Tortillas

Chad P. Shepherd

It was the second week of June in 2012. Our family was a full year away from moving to Guatemala, but I packed up my oldest, Caleb, age 12, and he and I went with a small team to build a house for a mother and her two children in the village of Cerro Alto, Guatemala.

Caleb was amazing that week, his contributions growing with his experience. First climbing a tree and watching the village, then helping to stoke wood fires, and finally joining the young boys with their games in the dirt, and even the teams with the construction of the wood framed house. By day three, he was down from that tree and already learning the language that he'd master in the years to come.

We finished the work that week, dedicated the house, and handed the key to the single mom who was raising an infant and a young girl. Mercedes would awaken at dawn each morning, courtesy of local roosters, and she'd first make a trek to carry back the day's firewood on her head, stacked on a small pile of rags. She'd get the fire started, and then while it burned, she'd make another hike down the mountain to gather water for the day. By the time the sun was shining, she was prepared to begin her day's preparation of their primary nutrition for the day, corn tortillas.

This would be her ritual every day before she would join into the hard labor of constructing a home while keeping her infant swaddled on her hip. At the end of the week, we watched and cried while she unlocked a door for the first time in her life and led her children into their first home. Little beds, stuffed animals, a kitchen table, and a door that locked... these were all firsts for them, and each little detail was a new chance at a better life. For the first time ever, that night they were guaranteed to be dry and to be safe.

Caleb and I boarded our flight the next morning and returned to the pace of our first world life.

One year later we would return with our entire family. We'd sold and donated everything we had, reducing our belongings to only what would fit into the maximum requirements of the airlines: twosuitcases and one carry-on per person... a total of 15 items. It was 13 really, because that included a Pack 'n Play and a stroller.

Our little family, three kiddos, Caleb age 13, Aleksandra age 10, and Sterling age one... we made our way back to Cerro Alto to lead a team and to build two more houses. What an experience this was with our newly adopted baby from China. We certainly didn't disclose that to the Chinese officials during our exit interview! They couldn't know that we were pastors and missionaries.

And so we worked the week and completed the houses. New dedications, new families under roofs, new keys placed in hands.

During the final prayer of the final home, while I had my eyes closed, suddenly a small and rough hand grasped my own. I opened my eyes and I gasped. It was Mercedes, and her baby was a year bigger, still swaddled to her side!

She had come and found me. She began tugging at my hand as she said, "Vámonos!" My feet followed her and I was delighted to see that she led me to her house, the very place where I had been one year before with my son. Her fire was burning and a steel plate was over the top of the flames. Her house had been painted a deep and beautiful blue, and she had built herself a small hutch filled with chickens. The door of the house opened and out walked her daughter, smiling and laughing!

Mercedes reached into a bucket and scooped out a handful of corn that had been smashed and mixed with water. She asked me if she could cook me a tortilla. Enthusiastically I said, "Yes!" And so a year ago this would have been a tortilla made by a lady who slept on a clay floor. The tortilla would have been made in her home of adobe brick and corn stalk walls. Now she did so outside of her secure home. The corn had been ground down by hand and had been grown on her own land. She cooked on open flames using wood that she had carried on her back up the mountain path.

She had no access to any type of healthcare, medicine, or financial support. Her family subsisted on about $5/ day. Even with all this hardship, she shared with me what she had with a smile.

Her hands began to pat the paste in her hands with practiced and expert skill. She rotated and flipped the batter as her hands continued to rhythmically pat, pat, pat. I was looking at the chickens in their pens when I heard the first sound from her mouth. Ptttt! It sounded like she spit. Hmm. Must have had something in her mouth. Maybe a fly was buzzing her. And then she spit again. My mouth dropped open as I watched the operation.

Open the palm of batter, a puff of spit from her mouth into the batter, pat-pat-pat, spit, flip and rotate, pat-pat-pat, spit, flip and rotate, and so on. All between big smiles on her face and the hopeful little face of her daughter, sweet little Kendra. All I could do was smile back as my mind freaked out and tried to think of a way to escape. Surely I could not eat this spit-made tortilla!

Then she held it out to me with the most beautiful smile I have ever seen. It was the moment of truth. Mercedes' eyes were locked onto me, her baby strapped to her hip, her gorgeous little daughter beside us. The chickens clucked in the pen and a breeze blew soft across the mountainside.

I took that tortilla. It was warm and it represented the sacred relationship that existed between me and my son and this woman and her children. We had shared a week on this land, and together we'd built a home and extended hope. I bit deep into that tortilla and ate it and the next two that followed. I will confess that I was also silently praying for my own well being!

Mercedes and Kendra were delighted. They asked if I'd brought my family, and I took the opportunity to tell them two things: (1) my family was here and I was going to go and get them, and (2) they'd already eaten and so she did not need to prepare tortillas for them! Moments later I returned with my family, and together we all celebrated Mercedes and her new life!

Mutual generosity made all the difference. It isn't so much about what you have to give; it matters much more that you simply give whatever you have.

I don't care where you decide to be generous. I don't care where you give. If you have a calling to help the homeless in America, then do it. If you have a desire to serve the destitute in India, then do it. If your neighbor is without healthcare, then spend your money to buy him what he needs. Our daily challenge is the same wherever we are... be a force of good. Live out your belief.

46

No Trespassing

CHAD P. SHEPHERD

"Not I, nor anyone else, can travel that road for you. You must travel by yourself. It is not far. It is within reach. Perhaps you have been on it since you were born and did not know. Perhaps it is everywhere - on water and land." —Walt Whitman

We were on a beach vacation at Holmes Beach, Florida in the summer of 2018. We navigated the local bus system to arrive at the pier late in the evening. We'd been looking forward to walking out to the end all day. Finally the air brakes hissed, the doors swung open, and we bounded out to the boardwalk. Our faces fell. "No Trespassing, Anyone trespassing on this property shall be guilty of a felony."

The night had been perfect to this point. The setting sun was dancing on the water and the seagulls had been replaced by bats snatching mosquitoes in the warming street lights. The airbrakes of the bussed hissed before I could hear its tires crunching gravel as it crawled away into the shadow of the city. The night seemed perfect for a bit of rule-breaking. Sure, some trespassing is illegal, but what about when rightful territory has been seized?

Aren't all the great breakthroughs of history a sort of trespassing? A disregard of stated barriers to reach a new discovery, a new land, or a new people? You may have heard people say something like, "Well, God shut that door and so I knew that this just wasn't his plan for my life."

Phooey on that! Closed doors might mean that you need to remove the entire wall. Open floor plans are better. There will always be barriers! When the Son of God came in the form of a man, He went about taking back territory, reclaiming lives, and reclaiming what was rightly his with every footstep. The barriers of the enemy were no match for his disregard of their signposts.

He is the God who shuts the mouths of lions, drops giants with a stone, parts the waters, flattens city walls, wipes out armies by lamplight and a shout, and who walks within the fiery furnace. He is the God who meets us on the battlefield and forgives us even as He hangs on a cross.

He is the God who makes a way, even when there seems to be no way. When we walk with him, nothing is bigger.

God can make a way from our brokenness. Those hard experiences that we remember can prepare you to face greater things ahead. When we know where we've come from, who created us, and what we've already overcome, then we can rip down the "No Trespassing" sign that seeks to block our way.

So did Aleksandra and I hop that fence? It would be an admission of a felony if I said that we did, and so I'll leave it to you to guess. There are barriers that should remain uncrossed. The wisdom is discerning the difference.

Perhaps you've been on a journey since you were born? Walk with God and claim your territory. You can't trespass on your Father's land.

47

WHO WAGS THE DRAGON'S TALE?

NANCY HULSHULT

W ith its 318 curves on an 11-mile highway in Tennessee, the legendary "Tail of the Dragon" was calling me. My husband Darrell and I had rented Harley motorcycles on vacation and took in the sights and smells of the autumn countryside with all the oranges, reds, and yellows mixed into the greenery of the mountains. It was our first time riding together, since there's just one Harley in our garage at home. I had so much fun that I suggested that we take on the infamous "Tail of the Dragon" as a highlight to our day. I had heard so much about the challenges and excitement of the winding road that I wanted to add this experience to our not-so-adventurous life. With some reservation, Darrell agreed.

As we rode closer to the area, the number of cyclists increased, and I secretly was jazzed by the Harley hand wave from other bikers. I started to feel pretty cool, like I actually fit into this scene and the scenery. We stopped at a Harley Davidson store for a break before tackling the Dragon, and then I shoved my helmet back on my head, pulled on my leather gloves, and swung my leg over my bike. I was ready for the roar of my bike and the roar of the Dragon. I was the dragon slayer that was going to ride the beast the full 22 miles, up and back for the full 638 curves. What a rush! What fun to share with my best friend!

As we rode the road that led to the Dragon, I could see the signs up ahead. Here we go! I was following Darrell, so I was comfortable that if he could navigate the curves, then so could I. Drawing closer to the Tail, the other bikers began to get crazy, passing me over the double yellow line at breakneck speed on the two-lane curves with mountain rock overhead, and then sliding between Darrell and me. On some curves, I lost track of Darrell and wondered whether or not I could continue on this treacherous path. Between the loose gravel on the side of the road and the double yellow, I stayed the course and prayed, "Help me, Jesus!" Then it happened.

The rain. It just didn't start with a sprinkle; it fell like a drenching curtain, every drop smacking the shield of my helmet so much so that I had to physically wipe the shield of my helmet, wishing it had windshield wipers. The downpour hit sharply through my leather jacket and stung through my denim jeans. I didn't want to stop because I knew Darrell was ahead of me, perhaps thinking that I would catch up soon. Suddenly my thrill-seeking sense of adventure seemed more like a fool's fatally flawed recipe for disaster.

I no longer wanted to ride the Tail of the Dragon. I didn't want the braggery or the T-shirt. I didn't care if I went home with my own tail between my legs. I wanted off, and wanted off now!

Soon I caught sight of Darrell's motorcycle at one of the few pull offs with enough room between the road and the cliff to turn around. Darrell was facing back the way we had come and motioned that we were going back the way we had come. Carefully, I made the U-turn and watched for a safe time to pull back on the road. We rode through the rain for about 2 miles before the rain stopped. We rested, soaking wet, in the parking lot of the Harley Davidson shop, feeling so defeated. The Dragon whipped us with the tip of his tail before we could even get a good grip on him. It wasn't even a fight; it was surrender, a surrender to nature, to the elements.

In the shop, I decided to buy a T-shirt that boasted images of the dragon, as though I had conquered it. It is more of a testimony about God saving me from myself, my ego, my false bravery. It reminds me that my idea was foolish, that I was not prepared for what lay ahead, and that God had something better for me. He sent me the torrential rain, the harbinger of nature to avoid disaster and to get me to stop and redirect my path.

Amazingly, as soon as Darrell and I started our journey back, we noticed that the roads were dry, there were no clouds in the sky, and the sun was shining again. All the rain was behind us. We enjoyed the rest of our day on scenic roads with just a few nice curves and hardly any other traffic to come between us.

But I kept thinking about that dragon, how I wanted to conquer it, and how God called a truce between us on that day by sending the rain. The battle was not a necessary one to be fought on that day.

Why does a dragon wag its tail? "Tail wagging in a lizard, like a dragon or monitor or skink, usually means it's displaying it's alert and perhaps really enjoying something it's doing (usually seen when eating). Apr 17, 2019 Wikipedia So, enjoy the truce today, dragon. I lived another day for the real battles in my life, the spiritual ones.

I read about the dragon in Scripture and I think about Revelation 12:9 (NIV), "The great dragon was hurled down—that ancient serpent called the devil, or Satan, who leads the whole world astray. He was hurled to the earth, and his angels with him." We constantly engage in the spiritual battle on earth until our last day on earth when God reclaims us and ultimately will claim victory over Satan and death forever.

This Scripture is also a favorite of Chad Shepherd, as he believes that it is "one of the timeless passages that has been historically true, is true now, and will be true in the future. GOD is not limited by linear time and his I AM status is not easily comprehended. Theologians argue over this passage. Was it referring to ancient Babylon, or metaphorical for the time of John's writing, written to get word out to the followers of Christ from his banishment at Patmos, future based on the culmination of all things, or was it a literal telling of an actual angelic war in heaven?

"My answer to this debate is yes. It is. This is a timeless telling of what was true, is true, and forever will be true... outside of time and over context.

"Yes. The mother in the passage was going to have the child devoured, she was unable to stop it. She merely held her ground. God got the victory, but she was faithful.

"Sometimes... God lets me get eaten. It is only after I'm in the belly of the beast that I realize God gave me a knife, that is, the Sword of the Spirit. It is then that I began to cut my way out from the inside? Like Daniel IN the lion's den, the three Hebrew children IN the furnace, Moses IN the desert, the disciples IN the storm.... In this world you will have trouble, but take heart for I have overcome the world....

"And I had it all along, like Dorothy with her ruby slippers. If only I had recognized it and let it do its work."

Yes, on this earth in spiritual warfare, sometimes we whip the Dragon; sometimes the Dragon whips us. But in heaven, we will celebrate victoriously with the One who overcomes all evil and wins the eternal battle for our souls.

48

Why the Wheels?

Nancy Hulshult

People often ask why I love to ride my motorcycle. I can't explain it, just like I can't explain the smell of spring or fall, refreshing wind that blows straight into my face, the roar of the Harley motor in my ears, or the aromatic flavors of every passing restaurant as I head toward the winding country roads. I take in the odor of the farmland with freshly bundled hay mixed with the smell of wildflowers and cow manure. It's all part of becoming one with the real world, the one without air conditioning and fake car deodorizers that dangle from car mirrors. It's all natural and all so personal. Just me on a bike just following the two-lane roads to nowhere. To have no destination, no map, no time constraints, if only for one Saturday morning when life has given me a reprieve from responsibility, other than to be keenly aware of my surroundings, for my pleasure and for my safety. My only prayer that comes to mind frequently is, "Thank you, Jesus!"

If I want to really pray and slow life down a bit, I enjoy a long bicycle ride through the canopy of woods on the bicycle trail in Oregonia, Ohio. I know where to put in and where to get off. I know that regardless of the temperature or humidity, The trees covering the path keep the ride enjoyable. I have the time and the balance to look to the sides of the trail and enjoy the squirrels and the birds, the wild violets and black-eyed susans. The quiet of the ride allows me to think, to reflect, and to dream ahead to what God may have for me next. He reminds me of challenges in life when I have to rise to a stand and pump the pedals to get up the next hills, as well as the blessings of life that let me cruise downhill without expending a single bit of energy. Even the level pathways remind me to keep on course and enjoy the ride.

If I think about where my love for wheels began, I remember the tricycle that had a stand on the back to carry my little brother down the sidewalk before he learned to ride. I remember the confusion of the bicycle with training wheels as I rocked back and forth until

I got the hang of keeping both of them off the ground. I remember my dad running behind me to steady my bike until I could ride on my own. The sweetest victory was the feel of freedom when I finally chucked the training wheels and took off on my own two wheels. From there I could explore entire neighborhoods away; I could exercise my independence and gang up with other friends to ride...just ride.

Perhaps some day, sooner than I wish, I'll be in some semblance of wheels, in a wheelchair or stumbling along with a walker with two front wheels. I'll be dependent on other things and other people for mobility. So for now, when folks ask why I ride, I really can't explain it.

235

49

Fresh Air

Chancey Bosch

I have been awake since 3:10am, tossing in my bed at a pace just slower than the rustling of the wind outside the window. My mind is chasing the power of nature, the modeling, foreshadowing, and mentoring it does in our lives. I'm drawn back to what can sound like a fictional Hallmark setting, and what can seem like a light dream. But this is no dream. This is no story. This was a summer that changed many things, too many things perhaps. In fact, it was this past summer.

Driving through upstate New York with my home five states in the rear view, I'm just now starting to breathe and think. It has been a long year at work, full of demands, deadlines, and devils. Well, that was just an alliteration to highlight the politics of dealing with people who don't really care about me or my future. I have a pattern of sacrificing too much for other people's work, and I was beginning to let myself think about changing jobs.

That line of thinking usually leads me back to the only one job I left prematurely. I was teaching at a school in Hamilton, Ohio. More important than the place were the people. It was a school called H.O.P.E, led by one of my favorite bosses ever, Nancy Hulshult. At that time, I needed H.O.P.E. as much as my community and my soon to be students. Nancy and I shared a common purpose and common goals. Behind the veil of curriculum and classroom management, metal detectors and rules, students and teachers, was a belief that the light of hope was Jesus. Further, the light in H.O.P.E. would be people bringing love and understanding to our students. I left in chase of something new, something closer to family, and a naivete that this type of work and leadership was everywhere.

Back to the story. The road is in front of me, and the sun is beaming through the windows in a deceptive way: the way that tricks you into thinking it's 102 degrees outside when it's a perfect 74. I crack the windows to help cycle the air. Little did I know, nature is back at it, foreshadowing and modeling what is about to happen. As the cooler air pushes the hot air out, my senses shift to my sight.

I've almost missed the fact that I am in the Catskills, passing the Finger Lakes, and surrounded by trees, trees, and more trees. Driving just over the speed limit, I feel as if I can't find the end to this beauty. There is a feeling of foreverness, a feeling that the next turn is undefined, unknown, and undisturbed. It's a random midweek day at 2pm, so for all I can see, I am the only one that really exists out here.

The sight, sound, and feel of nature around me has had an effect on my feelings, and it's starting to have an effect on how I think. I've always seen the physical world as something to watch. I'm a researcher, a learner, a reader, and a teacher. Leadership principles, human interaction, systems thinking...these all find a philosophical home in nature. Today is going to be a reminder of that.

I start to think about the pressure of work, the unending demands of others, the reports, the meetings, the grandstanding, the rules, the hypocrisy, the fears...a forest of organizational monotony. Ah, the trees! The trees seem to never stop. They are individual tasks that seem achievable until they stand together. I don't know what I'm talking about, but I can feel it. There is an unknowable boundary that is seen and felt. But why is that depressing, and the Catskills refreshing?

A Finger Lake. I can catch a glimpse; a quick detour is all I need. I have to see it; I have to mark it off a list. But it gives more to me than I was willing to give to it. I've grown up around lakes, never understanding why Michigan's motto isn't the Land of 1,000 Lakes. I have family with a lake house. My favorite moments have been on lakes and boats. This all comes rushing back to me, but in a deeper sense. These Lakes sitting before me have a depth, a stillness, a firmness, a calmness. In the midst of a forest sits a natural reservoir of a different sort.

I start to think about how the trees, the lakes, the hills, all work together, and I might as well be in 3rd grade learning about land formation and the water cycle again. But it all seems new somehow. What is this telling me? I don't know, I'm confused...I just drive.

The constant trees, open air, slightly winding turns and rolling hills keep the landscape before me neat and clean, somehow putting a new canvas in front of my thoughts. I start to ask questions. Why do I have to go back to work? Why do I have to even leave New York? Why can't I just stay here? My wandering soul gets the best of me, and I start to think about what jobs I could get here. Everyone needs a teacher; that'd be easy. Maybe there is a local college, a regional campus for the State University...which just happens to be called SUNY.

It hits me like a ton of bricks. I still have a wife, a home, a cat, a whole life five states back. I'm not trying to escape that, but what I see and feel is telling me something. It is starting to emerge. One part of me wants what I can't have. I want the trees, hills, and lakes back home in Oklahoma. Well, we have a saying for that: "The grass is always greener on the other side." One look at a cow in a field, and nature starts talking back to me again. But I'm in New York and it's talking to me.

I'm approaching the east coast; the landscape is changing slowly; but I can't let this slip by me. Why? Why this experience? Why everything? Well, that's too much. Maybe just why did this hit me so hard today?

I think it was the conversation that was intertwined throughout the entire trip, but specifically these last 200 miles. I wasn't just asking myself those questions, and I wasn't throwing them against the inside of the windshield. I have another philosophical underpinning, and that is there is a God who is and does. My thoughts have been a conversation all day long. One with answers... answers in the language of sight, sound, emotion, and thoughts. A language of nature.

So how did I interpret them? Well, I'm writing this four months after the fact. I have a new job, a new boss, a new demand, new pressures....well, new trees. There's another organizational forest. But this is no mistake. This is not a decision gone bad. That's what I learned. That's the conversation I was having in the midst of being overwhelmed, undervalued, and unfulfilled. It took a long drive through Upstate New York to see the trees in spite of the forest.

There are always more trees, more hills, more lakes, new days, new tasks, new jobs. The idea that we are contained by the moment, by our routine, by the expectations upon us, by the future decided for us...this is artificial. This is the idea that my summer drive shattered. There's no problem with opening the window, letting in fresh air, letting nature talk to you, talking to the One Who Is and asking what can be. For me, it was affirmation of something new. Nature is always new!

241

50

His Story is Our Story

Chad P. Shepherd

I it was August of 1992 when I left home. I shifted my 1978 avocado green Buick Skylark into drive, the truck full of clothes, supplies, and a few furnishings for my dorm room at Anderson University, exactly 100 miles east of my childhood home. My Papaw, Pop, was riding shotgun and my mom and Mamaw Mathis were in the new Lincoln behind me. I'd said goodbye to Dad in the driveway, he was left behind because he had to work. My mother didn't tell me how devastated he was when I left until this year when my daughter left for that same university. I cried for a week.

The summer of 1992 was different, I shed no tears. I had big dreams and planned to go and re-shape the world. Pop fell asleep along the way; I think he had carcolepsy, a fictitious disease that causes one to fall asleep whenever riding in a car. Two hours later, when I exited the interstate, my right tires drifted over to the rumble strip and he awoke with a shock, feet kicking the bottom of my dashboard and hands banging off of the headliner! I couldn't help but laugh, and then felt instantly bad about it and told him I was sorry.

I had done it. I'd escaped Preble County. Several major changes later, a wedding, graduation, and then off to live life. Over the next 24 years we'd move 15 times, travel the world, have and adopt babies, see miracles, have multiple career changes, do some really great things, and then crash and burn it all. She and I sat in a coffee shop in August of 2019 and made choices that led to divorce in March of 2020, the year of the pandemic.

Later we learned that four other missionary families who we worked with in Guatemala had also returned to the U.S. and divorced. That information was both devastating and oddly also made me feel like I wasn't alone. Still, I nearly lost my mind that year. The isolation of living alone when the kids were with their mother; the silence was maddening. I was a man who had chosen to lose it all and I had no hope for the future. Each day was simply a routine to get through the night. I felt ashamed and humiliated. Pastors and missionaries should not get divorced. I'd failed.

I got a dog and I went to see a therapist. I told God that I was done with him. I agreed that he existed and I wasn't going to turn away from him, but... I wasn't going to give a penny to a church or to missions. I wasn't going to volunteer or even tell anyone that I'd been a pastor. I was done! I got more tattoos, changed my style to look rougher, grew my hair out long, and wore a scruffy beard. Leave me alone, God, and for sure leave me alone, Christians! But God did not abandon me.

To my immense frustration and nervous laughter, people walked up to me over and over, asking me a single question. "Are you a pastor?" Are you kidding me? I'd respond the same each time, "Do I look like a pastor?" The response was always a variant of the same, "Um, well, no, but there's just something about you that I couldn't get away from. I feel like you're a pastor and I'm meant to talk to you." UGH. And so while I was attempting to hide from God, he'd send people to tell me their troubles: in parks, on trails, in stores, at work, on Facebook... I could not escape.

I'd pray with people and sometimes even lead them to a deeper level of faith. All the while, I was feeling worthless and broken and empty. After two years, while healing is happening in my life, God continues to hijack my days with unlikely conversations and inexplicably observant passersby who somehow sniff out the clergy in me. It got to the point that I finally literally threw up my hands like Pop hitting my headliner and exclaimed, "Fine! What do you want from me, God?"

And so now here I am. Lord. Send me. Where, I don't know. To do what? I have no idea. But, like Jonah who took a three day ride in a big fish, I cannot hide from God. Grace is real. Second chances are real. I'm done trying to shape my life. I've made choices that are irrevocable and now all I have is today and this moment. Somehow that has become enough. Sometimes, just barely enough. I still have days that swallow me. But, I am here to tell you that God is who he says he is. He really does love us. He is not far from us. And his story is our story.

51

Waving Trees

Chancey Bosch

Irented a cabin in the Ozark Mountains to escape all the things I work so hard to create. These things aren't the types of problems you complain about in public, or even to your friends. Instead, they are the things our social, psychological, and fiscal structures encourage us to create. It's the job with just enough demands to be too demanding. It's the schedule with just enough events to be unmanageable. It's the right amount of friends, diversified over different small communities, that makes being a good friend unachievable. It's the pursuit of more that leaves you with less. Overall, it's the self-care that doesn't really deliver on caring for the self. I may be a prisoner of my own design. I have been two days in a rustic cabin with coffee, a fire to keep going, and an almost endless pile of snacks, perhaps a metaphor to the endless piles of paperwork I want to escape. I guess I thought I was hungry when I bought all of this junk food. What is more important, though, is what I don't have with me: my work computer, my phone, my work phone, media, social media, or even books.

My mind is starting to find a less heightened sense of being on overload – the type of overload that makes one feel underwhelmed with life and with oneself. It's early, no need for a clock, so it's somewhere between dark and light. The fire is lit, somewhere between flickering and inflamed. The fire is started but not stable; it is working on finding a way. The flames bounce from one side of the log to the other. At one moment it seems strong, and the next it struggles. Time gives the fire its power. The fire heats the seasoned logs, and eventually the fire is feeding itself. From ember to log, the heat is beginning to move through the small room. The flame is beginning to reduce my anxiety, worries, and fears. It is drawing me in, drawing me down into myself. Fortunately for me, the rocking chair is next to the fire, angled to give me a view of both the fire and back window with a simple shift in gaze.

The sky is turning from dark black to gray. The landscape begins to transform from an abyss of gray into shades of brown and gray in the shape of hills, trees, limbs, and the few leaves refusing to let go of summer. It's these shapes that begin to bend my mind and thinking. The slow burning fire seems to foreshadow the hot embers of contemplation being blown on by the landscape before me. The landscape seems to have a breath to it. It is breathing life into my thoughts by its movement. These are the large exhales from nature into my distant self that seem to fulfill the foreshadowing of the slow fire next to me. It is as if things are happening in me, next to me, and beyond me.

In total, four things are speaking to me: the dancing fire, the waving trees, the fluttering leaves, and my bouncing foot. The trees wave with long, slow hands like a castaway getting the attention of a plane 30,000 feet in the air. I guess nature is trying to bring my attention back to the moment, the present. As I participate with nature's gesture and narrow the distance between my thoughts and the moment, I begin to notice the leaves fluttering at a faster pace than the waving trees. If they had an emotional expression, they would be smiling. In the foreground, I even notice that my foot has stopped bouncing with anxiety. Unintentionally, my breath begins to slow, my thoughts become grounded, and I cast my gaze back into the fire.

For a short moment, my thoughts, my life, my anxieties creep back into the driver's seat. I wish I could take all of that stuff and stick it in the fire. I bounce my eyes back to the landscape, my thoughts follow, and I take a deep breath to try to relax and not think. Too quickly I start thinking about not thinking, and my foot starts to bounce again. Soon the family awakens, the fire needs stoking, the view is in the full sun, and those precious moments that were just mine are gone. Wait, I have one more day, one more morning, one more chance to see and feel all of this again.

I wake up early the next morning, the last morning. I am

anticipating more arm waving and hand flapping from nature. Fire started, coffee in hand, darkness giving way to dawn. Nothing. There's nothing. The same landscape that spoke to my soul yesterday is present, but absent of animation. No movement, no slight sway, nothing. It seems so simple. Was it just the wind? But it's never just wind, trees, leaves, or fire. Perhaps it is the weather. Perhaps it has nothing more to say until I am ready to listen. It must be the old "teacher will appear when the student is ready" maxim. I think that's how nature is. If I were ready, I'd probably see something new today, but I'm fixed on yesterday. For now, that's okay with me. I have much to think, learn, and do.

In reflection, I'm not sure if I solved anything these last few days: no existential changes, no epiphanies, no eureka moments. However, I did find a bit of peace and clarification. Parts of me did burn in that fire. These parts must be small because I'm still me, going back to the job, home, friends, and schedule I left two days ago. However, it may be the small parts, the bits of me that were burned away, purified, or survived during the intense fire of contemplation that has changed me. At minimum, moments of anxiety were burned away. At maximum, my soul caught rhythm with the invisible: the wind, a breath, and a voice. It's a wind because it animates things, it's a breath because it gives life, it's a voice because it speaks. In rhythm, my soul danced with a guiding newness of love.

This dance, the invisible, is what I choose to take with me when I leave the cabin. It's the lesson that I take when I return to the suburbs, the 50-hour weeks, the endless issues. The invisible is the qualitative sixth sense that says things are not what you think. It's the conviction that when we are trapped inside our circumstances, we can reach out to the natural world around us and let it wrestle with the world within us. Maybe this is what it's like to wrestle with the angels, to be touched, and to be changed. The lesson can't be found in a standard, objective, or goal. It's not something I can show and tell; it's something I'm challenged to be. It may be invisible to me and others, but it's not imperceptible.

There are landscapes around us that we ignore, both within and without. Although the invisible is unknowable, except as a proximate knowing, nature waits and welcomes me into truth limited. This invisible truth is always wanting to be sensed, wanting us to sense. It carries smells. It carries air. It has a place. It pushes against us. It animates stillness. It howls through space. It's palpable. I don't think God is the wind, but the wind informs me of God. God informs the wind. Nature informs me. God informs me. How? Well, I hope you can carve out some space to go to a place where nature will speak to you personally. I trust this is not unique to me. Be encouraged, the trees are waving.

52

WALKING ON

NANCY HULSHULT

"When I was a young boy, I mounted a horse to go for a ride, and the horse took off running. I held on tightly to that horse and never let go."

Mark is our neighbor, who has worked 30 years to restore his land back to the way it was, free of invasive species of plants. He tells us of a small herd of horses that run freely on his grounds and of the wildlife that are rarely seen: bobcats, 12-point bucks, coyotes, and the like. Two hundred year old trees provide a canopy of shade and protection, and Elk Creek flows freely with cold water. Years ago, Shawnee used small arrowheads to hunt elk, black bear, mountain lion, and bobcats to feed their families.

Mark is an engaging storyteller, a descendant of the Chickamauga of the Cherokee tribe. The Cherokee, who lived in Ohio for years, fought with Puxamo trying to preserve their land. Married into a family owning large estates in the area, Mark strives to preserve the land and the heritage of his indigenous people. He has worked for 30 years to remove invasive species of plants in order to return the land to what it once was. He and his sons, Joshua, Jamie, Steven and Matthew would come home from work and go into the woods every day to remove honeysuckle. Today one can look deep into the woods at the tall trees, standing straight and sturdy, freed from the entangling underbrush and roots of pervasive intruders.

A son and grandson of Baptist preachers, Mark says that he loves Jesus Christ and God, the Father and Creator of all life. He proudly quotes the great leader Puxamo from a speech recorded in ink as a guide for his people

"Today we stand here, my red children, listen to me, for the Creator, Gitchemonitou, is watching over us. He has a great stick. On the end of the stick, he has taken spider webs and has made a big net, and on the last day on Turtle Island, the last day that we are here, if you have done good, if you have treated your children good, if you have went out and brought the four-legged kind and the fish, and the edible plants and the medicine plants home for your children and the elders, and you have not laid with another's wife in her wigwam, if you have not sown discord, if you have done good, on the last day, he will reach down and swoop you up to be with him. But woe unto you, my red children, of Gitche matchitou, which is underground, if you have broken these ways, if you have sown discord, if you have laid out and you have not hunted and fished and brought down these animals and brought them home and fed them to the elders who can't hunt for themselves, if you have not fed these little children that cannot feed themselves, woe to you. He also has a big stick with spider webs in a big net, and he will reach up and bring you down to be underground in darkness. You will never have a chance to be close to Gitche manitou ever, for you will live in darkness with him. So make your decisions well."

Then Mark said, "God created nature for all races of people. We came from the 12 tribes of Israel. Native Americans knew to plant gardens for six years, then move it, and let the land restore itself.

"We get to live here for free. God created it for us. God owns the earth, except for the prince of principalities, but we have to pay taxes to Caesar. When the natives lived here, the love of the land was not over what it could produce. They knew they got to live here, so they were grateful and thankful and treated the land with respect.

"Woe to those inhabitants who use the land up until there is nothing left.

"In 1926 the native people were allowed to become American citizens, and in 1979, allowed to practice the freedom of religion. 1979!

"How did they practice their religion? All my people were southern Baptist preachers. They had their own government; they had their own stores; they had their own homes; they did basket

255

weaving and raised hogs; everything they were against just to become accepted. Then in 1839, they won the right to stay on their land through the Supreme Court under Andrew Jackson. They were the only ones in the United States to win. Yet, they still lost and had to go to Oklahoma. All tribes had to walk, not just the Trail of Tears. Here the Shawnees had to go to Lebanon, and then walked to Kansas."

"Shawnees came up from Tennessee because they had been fighting among themselves. Several tribes ended up in Ohio, including Shawnee, Wyandot, Delaware, Seneca, Miami by 1795. It was dangerous to live here.

"On this land, some people said they were brutal. But if you think about it, if you owned your house and lived in it, you might have to kill people, dismember them, and hang them up to try to discourage them. They had their own systems set up. If you were caught in adultery, you were flogged; and the second time, you were disbanded, death. Misbehavior was disruptive and disrespectful to the Creator, Gitchi Manitou. How can you lie and do these things in front of the Creator, the King, the Chief?

"Not all of the settlers were bad. The natives saw that the mothers and fathers and children were good people.

"But the military wanted the land and the trees. After 1776, they were promised land from the government, so the natives had to go."

"War was different with the natives. They would fight amongst each other, but they would only kill a couple and quit. They didn't know the European kind of war where you kill everybody and burn everything. They didn't do that. It was more about pride, who was the toughest, and they knew when to quit.

"The settlers came in and ringed the trees...chopped all around to kill it because they couldn't chop them down. They were too big. Then they planted their crops. Thistle started to come up. Before that, there were parakeets flying all around (in Ohio). The settlers killed all the parakeets and ate them. The parakeets would eat the thistle; then the ones that were left started eating their apple seeds, so the settlers killed them. They ate most of the box turtles and pileated woodpeckers and killed most of them. They called them flying chickens. My dad ate them, too. There is also a bigger woodpecker called the ivory billed.

"On the land is evidence of the Shawnee tribe, who once inhabited our land and left evidence of their existence: artifacts in the creek and a prayer wheel of rocks in the woods. The prayer wheel looks like a wheel, a circle of rocks with a cross in the middle. The four big rocks indicate the four directions, the four winds, the four ways, and in the middle you have a center rock, and that represents Gitchi manitou; and over here there was a smaller rock, nobody could really say what they rock was for, but I was told it was to represent the Son, and the Creator, he had a son.

"You go to that wheel, and you got your tobacco and you go up there and offer tobacco, and you say, 'Gitchi manitou, I am so sorry for what I've done; I've done wrong. I've not gone and got animals, I have not gone and got plants, and I have not done these things. I am very sorry. I'll change my ways.' The four elders present would hear your words, and if you did not honor your promise to the Great Creator, you would be whipped for your failure to honor the One who gave you life. The Creator gives you all you need for free: the animals to eat, the fish to eat, the birds to eat, the ground to plant their corn, squash. The creek down here, the water, it's all free. And yet you want to disrespect and act like a heathen. God's the king; he's the chief; you will respect him."

According to Mark, William Henry Harrison (9th U.S. president) and Tecumseh were here. They walked the land, and Harrison told Tecumseh, "We're here to stay. We're like the sands of the sea and the leaves of the tree. You might as well get used to it."

Mark: "Shawnee leader Tecumseh and his people said, 'Why do

you have to have everything? We know we're defeated people. Why can't we just have a little bit in Ohio?' But no, out they went. The government drove them out, and they couldn't understand that: 'You say that you love God. You say you love Jesus Christ. You say all these things, but you do all these bad things. Isn't it written in your book to do good things?'

"People coming in, destroying everything, taking everything, our ways, they didn't know.

If you love Jesus, why did you kill him? Why'd you do all those things before you killed him? He was a great chief. If Jesus had been here, he would have been honored!"

The pioneers also left evidence of grave markers of large rocks set upright to honor their dead. Local folklore suggests that no human blood was shed on our property, but the land served different races of people at different times with crops, deer, birds, and other wildlife to feed their families. Today our hope is to preserve the land, the animals, and the birds for future generations.

We believe that the Holy Spirit of the Great Creator is still here on the land. In honor of the great chief, Jesus Christ, this land is preserved for people to come and feel the presence of God in nature. In the middle of all the beauty and history, one can pray, meditate, reconnect, recharge, and be restored.

Jesse Banks, Mark's dad, has walked on, but his legacy lives on through his son. With great respect, Mark says, "My people never say that someone has died. We say that my dad has walked on." Walking on. From his walk on the earth to his walk into the heavens with Gitchi manitou, Mark's father walks with God.

This powerful image is similar to the image of God walking with Adam and Eve in the Garden of Eden. Humans began their existence walking with God in the garden. When we leave earth, we will once again return to the perfect garden in the presence of God.

Our journey through life is a walk in physical form to a walk in the spiritual realm. We and our ancestors are all walking on, through history, through the natural realm, and through the spiritual realm, together with God. Known by many names, our God reigns in all the realms. To Gitchi manitou, God, Holy One, King, Great One, whatever the name, to God we give thanks and give the glory for our being.

53

Pride is a Good Way to Fall

Chad P. Shepherd

I remember posting on social media two songs that both boasted, "Let the storms come." I remember taunting the enemy of my soul, telling him, "Do your best, We won't move from this place. We are taking it to your gates." I didn't recognize the pride in my own heart. It was never us. It was always only God. My job then had only been to answer, "Yes." How did I get it so twisted that my humble "Yes, I am willing to give it all" turned into a foolish, "Bring it, Satan"?

Within six months I was bankrupt, exhausted, broken, and driving a van 2000 miles through Mexico to get back home and try to somehow put back together my life. Within three years I'd be out of ministry, separated from my wife, my family shattered by divorce. Satan was far stronger than I. I felt like Job who had everything quickly taken, except I was not innocent. I'd forgotten the stories that made me: the stories of my grandpa who turned a bear wrong-out-sidewards with his bare hand; a grandfather who fell on his knees daily to pray for me; Mamaw Elsie, Mack, and Ruth who hugged me and kissed me and guided me for so many years; the pastors that had counseled me, Mitchell, Tarr, Curtis, Montgomery, Hill, and Hutchinson. I was who I was because of the legacy that had carried me so far.

Once I found myself alone in a fourth floor apartment, I was stunned. I stood at a new balcony. It overlooked Carmel, Indiana and it was cold, vacant, heartless, without purpose, and I was alone. No mission. The only positive thing was that pride was vanquished. I suppose that was the first necessary step. The only thing keeping me alive was the knowledge that my death would cause exponentially greater distress to those I'd already harmed: my parents, my children, my ex-wife and my family through that now broken union. The only way forward for me was to move forward through the pain that I deserved to feel. I had to be a better man.

A better dad. A better son. A kinder man to Kellie. I breathed in the night sky over Carmel and found a single calming thought... I could be genuine. Real.

That was two years ago and it has been painful day after day. If I could time travel to myself a few years back, I'd plead with myself to do things differently. Do not give up on your marriage. Fight. Love your wife. Let go of your pride. Stop being selfish and remember again how to serve. Take the time to rest. You were burnt out. Stretched too thin. You lost sight. The wrongs that I saw that others had done to me could have simply been forgiven.

Recently the public healthcare company where I work held a coffee social where we could meet the executive staff. I had worked with the CEO of our company 25 years ago when she was a manager. I walked up to her, delicious coffee in hand and introduced myself. She smiled at me, extended her hand, and we began to chat. We rapidly caught up and exchanged stories. I felt really happy that she'd remembered me and thought maybe the conversation would help me advance within the company. It was at that moment that she delivered the bombshell that brought my mind rapidly through the past two decades and the folly of my own journey. "Chad, I've really enjoyed catching up with you. You seem much more at peace than you used to be, actually, quite a bit less arrogant. It was good catching up." Then she turned and walked away.

Far less arrogant.

Pride is a good way to fall. It seems that I needed to fall a little farther. I remembered my interactions with her so many years ago. I was a recent college graduate and I was passionately defending the position of my supervisor at the time who had been passed over for a promotion. I remember being aggressive in my argument and tactless. I acknowledged that my approach had indeed been arrogant... and then immediately I recognized arrogance in my work in Guatemala, and even arrogance as I stood at that balcony rail overlooking the city. None of it had been accredited to me.

Two balconies. One filled with pride, the other humility after a fall. The CEO was right. I was a better man now than I had been when I thought I was at the top of my world. The price that I had to pay to reach this realization was far too high. More than I can pay. Grace. Realization overcomes me that my only hope is the grace of God. It was always my only hope, but now I have landed firmly enough on my face to acknowledge it.

This Sunday I stood at church singing worship songs with tears in my eyes. This has been my practice for two years now. I go to church alone. I sit with strangers. I sit with families all around me. I sit in the 7th row, slightly stage right of center. My soul melts week after week, and in my brokenness, I weep and my soul worships. I raise my hands. I close my eyes. I seek what I had and lost. No one there knows who I am, what I did, or what I lost. This Sunday the lyrics pierced me. They spoke of how I can't always see it when God is working. The words that escaped my lips along with thousands of others said that when all I can see is the battle, God can see the victory.

I couldn't sing anymore because I was gasping for air. Could that really be a promise for me? The next song had words leaving my mouth that proclaimed that when I'm fighting, I'm fighting on my knees. Yes, that is a promise for me. I have been on my face so long that I didn't even realize that somehow I had risen to a prostrated reverence on my knees. My posture was no longer about grinding my face in the dirt, but it was about yielding to the One who offered grace. Hands that were fistfulls of dirt now were open palms raised to my Savior.

I'm still a mess. I'm so lonely. I feel so incomplete. Sometimes I panic. My heart races and it is hard to breathe. I don't want to die alone. Regret comes in overwhelming waves. The enemy of my soul covers me in guilt and shame. He tells me that there is no way up from this pit, but I've learned to grip the rails of my balcony and to sing praises. To give thanks. To drop to my knees and fight not with my own power, but in the humility that recognizes that it is God's grace that is enough here. Pride is a good way to fall. Humility is a good way to be lifted from your shattered state.

Meeting Nancy Hulshult and Mark Running Horse has been a healing action to my soul. Nancy and her husband Darrell have pulled me and my kids in like family. Hearing Mark Running Horse talk about walking on in the legacy of our forefathers and doing honor to the God who made us has quickened my own sense of legacy from my grandfathers. I think of Mark's description in the woods of taking the life of a deer by arrow. It is a tragedy. And yet out of that death, we give thanks and we acknowledge the sacrifice. We pledge that we move on from that place and honor the life and the loss and the pain.

This is where I find myself. It is time to get up from the facedown dirt stance. I rise again, a man who perhaps is a little less arrogant, ready to "walk on" from my past self at this point. I'm still in the battle, but I do believe that God sees a victory. I still can't fathom what that looks like. My soul still mourns. Even so, I believe that it exists.

54

The Legend and Legacy of Jesse Banks 1930-2015

By Mark Banks
as told to Nancy Hulshult

My dad Jesse Banks, the patriarch of the Banks' family Native American drum known as the Southern Singers, was our spiritual leader. He is the one who directed us on the journey that we took for 28 years. When he was living upon Turtle Island, he gave me the knowledge that I needed to take over the direction of our drum when he walked on into the spirit world six years ago. The directions that he had given me formed a path that I followed when he was living and still follow to this day. There is not one powwow, one school demonstration, library program, or for that matter, any diversity or inclusion program where I do not mention our leader and dad, Jesse.

The meaning of "walking on" is simply the passing, the stepping into the spirit world to be with the Creator. Since his walking on, I tell his children the things that he did, reminding the audience at the powwows of him, especially the patience that my dad had. Directions that he gave me were to direct this drum to keep our family, this inner circle, alive. I am to keep discord from our drum. The discord that others have tried in the public did not matter. For 28 years, for the public, we included them, never separated them, to always give the vision that we are all human, to always say that the Spirit has no color, to always clarify that children are the most important, the education of children, never to exclude them from our path and our journey. They will one day be the caretakers of our culture.

One time, my dad had said that our drum was sacred enough for our children to touch, for the children that know no hate, that know no anger, are the ones that we need to listen to. They will not complicate things as adults may do; they will only simplify them with our journey.

It has been such a great honor to walk in my dad's footsteps, to try to represent him. I would have followed my dad regardless of who he was. He was the one man that I knew did things in a good way, not only on the weekends, not only in front of crowds at diversity and inclusion programs, but daily he walked that path. For that, I am forever grateful to be a part of his life. He was such a great man that would take time at each gathering to talk to people, no matter how he felt that day, he would stop and talk to the people. He taught me to always leave their imagination of who we are, for that will instill in them to seek out who they are and how they can live. To be a part of the Native culture is to be included, to make one feel welcome, is what Dad taught me. It is such a great honor to have these memories of my dad.

My dad, Jesse Banks, came from the mountains, lived a life not so poor. He said that they had potatoes, they had gardens, and they had a mule. He said that his neighbors on the next mountain would come over and ask for the peelings of the potatoes. My dad said that in his eyes, they were rich. My dad lost his dad at the age of 39, a family that loved their father so much that my dad's brother grieved himself to death at the age of 6 over the loss of their father. This tells you the heritage of the relatives, my relatives, and what kind of men they were. They were a loving family that cared for their children and their family. Therefore, I know that my ancestors, my family, are looking down upon us, and they stand with smiles. They look down upon us and they are grateful for what we are trying to accomplish and carry on.

My father was not raised upon the reservation and was not raised with his people. He is a descendant of the Cherokee people from North Carolina. In his heart, in his path, he always lived native, such as gathering of the plants, the edible plants and the medicine plants, the taking of small game, rabbits and squirrels and game birds, always being grateful for the gifts that the Creator has given them. He once had told me that learning these traditions from his dad was one of the greatest memories of his life. His dad taught him how to track animals through the woods, how to set trotlines in the creek, how to snare the small game in the woods, learning their signs, learning the trails going through the woods, learning to look at leaves, branches, and twigs, whether they were disturbed, learning to train his eyes to pick up on this, to help better them to catch the game and to feed their family, and learning how to navigate the wilderness, putting out marks on trees, all such awesome feats to be taught.

When I became a young man, my dad taught me these things. He took me to the woods, and he taught me about the small game and what to look for. All these things, and the spiritual teachings that my dad has taught me, has left a great impression in my life. To keep my conscience alive is one of the most important things that Dad taught me, to keep it alive and to be aware of what I say and how I conduct myself. He said that if you get too confident in yourself, you could get hurt. Always be aware of what you say to people; always conduct yourself in a manner that would make them want to learn more about the culture.

My dad was an awesome teacher. People came from miles around to hear him speak because he would always include each individual as a human into the culture. The native spiritual aspect that I was taught didn't come until later in my life, but once I was taught the ceremonies and the traditions, I took it very seriously.

My dad would say, "Being a 'want-to-be' Indian is a good thing because they want to be, they want to help the people. They want to be a part of the culture and to feel wanted, to feel that they are doing good and helping the tribes.

In closing, I would like to say, my name is Mark Banks, the son of Jesse Banks. I would like to say thank you to my wife, Ann, for allowing me to go upon their land to conduct our ceremonies and our gatherings, the gathering at Killbuck Creek. I am trying to educate my grandchildren on the culture by teaching them the songs and the dances. I am trying my best to keep the culture alive, to walk that path that was taught to me. I will try not to be directed in any other way but the right way, to try not to let the distractions come into my life, which Gitchi matchitou, the dark angel, would try to do. I will do my best to educate these grandchildren of mine and to keep them involved.

Thank you very much, and may the Great Spirit be with you. Stahyu ("stay strong").

Jesse Dean Banks
(Photo by Alicia Fiddler, 2009)

Mark Banks
(Facebook profile photo-2009)

55

LOOK TO THE STARS

TYLER GREEN

I think it is fitting that my story is like many others. I grew up in a Christian home where my parents were faithful to our church and their Savior. Jesus was a constant theme in our home. Southern Gospel music, especially that of Sandi Patti, played on the radio in our kitchen. I had the privilege of watching my parents commit to raising their three children to love and follow Jesus. We sang in the choir, attended children's church, and went to VBS. My parents weren't perfect people, but they lived out their faith. We weren't wealthy by any means, but I never went without. My dad worked long hours in a factory so that my mom could stay home when we were young. I placed my faith in Jesus as a young child in my parent's bedroom. I didn't understand the deep things of Scripture, but I knew that I needed Jesus to forgive my sins. My mom prayed with me and led me to a saving relationship with Jesus. I grew up involved in church and was taught to love Jesus.

Then something shifted in my life. It wasn't subtle or the type of sin that creeps into your life when you are unaware. It happened in the hallway of my school during my 8th grade year. Two boys were talking in the hallway. To be honest, I don't even remember who they were. They were laughing about something in that crowded hallway when I walked up to them. One of the boys cursed and the other used that one word to mock me. He said, "Don't say that in front of Tyler. He is a Christian." I made a conscious decision at that moment to never let that happen to me again. I was determined to fit in. I wanted to belong. I wanted to impress those two boys and I couldn't do that if they thought of me as a Christian. The decision I made in that moment would shape the next six years of my life. It was a decision born out of my own insecurities.

It was a cool night and I could feel the wind blowing against my face. I was now twenty and had spent the last six years trying to find my place. Six years after that conversation in a junior high school hallway, I was no closer to understanding my calling or value. I was still running from God, my parents, and the person I knew I was called to be. I still longed to "fit in" and was more concerned with what my peers thought than what God wanted. I lit up my cigarette while standing behind my parents' house. Things at home had deteriorated to the point that my dad had asked me to move out. I was at a crossroads in my life.

We lived in the country away from all the lights of the city. There wasn't a cloud in the sky as I exhaled the smoke I had just pulled into my lungs. The smoke was dissipating into the air as I looked up into the sky. The stars stood out from the darkness of the universe that night, almost as if God made them a little more brilliant that night just for me. As I gazed into the heavens, God spoke to my heart. That moment is burned into my memory. It had been so long since I had heard from the Lord. The Spirit of God whispered into my heart that night, "I made all of this. You can't run from me." That was all God said to me that night. I didn't see a light or hear an audible voice. It was just God reminding me that of all the amazing things in creation, he still loved me. In the midst of my rebellion, sinful nature, selfishness, and disobedience, God still saw value in me.

It has now been almost 21 years since that moment in my parent's backyard. I still don't look at the stars the same. It was later that year that I rededicated my life to following Jesus. I had no idea what God wanted to do in my life that night. I had no desire to serve in a ministry role. I had no idea that weeks later I would quit smoking, walk away from friendships, and choose a different path in life. It would only be a few months later that I would meet the most beautiful redhead God ever created. Nine months after that, I would convince her to marry me. Twenty years of marriage and seven children later, I am aware that what I have been entrusted with today began that night, gazing into the heavens and being reminded that God was still pursuing me.

I don't know that any of us really ever conquer fear like the fear

I had as a 14-year-old boy. We want to be accepted, appreciated, and validated. Most of us could list off our weaknesses much quicker than our strengths. It is easy to become our own worst critic. We compare ourselves to others from a distance but use a microscope to dissect our every flaw. The truth is that I have been good at many things but never really terrific at anything. I'm not the most gifted in the things that the world celebrates. This has been true for me in ministry as well. I have had the honor of serving with people much more gifted than me in leadership. I led worship in our church for years knowing that I am not a gifted musician. I have friends who are amazing communicators, the type of people you could just sit and listen to. It can be hard for all of us, even pastors, to know how to find our place in a world that celebrates the gifts that we don't see in ourselves. It is why I still remember the stars that night.

In Scripture the stars, as well as all heavenly creations, are called to praise the Lord.

> Psalm 148:1 — "*Praise the LORD! Praise the LORD from the heavens; praise him in the heights!*"
>
> Psalm 148:2 — "*Praise him, all his angels; praise him, all his hosts!*"
>
> Psalm 148:3 — "*Praise him, sun and moon, praise him, all you shining stars!*"
>
> Psalm 148:4 — "*Praise him, you highest heavens, and you waters above the heavens!*"
>
> Psalm 148:5 — "*Let them praise the name of the LORD! For he commanded and they were created.*" (ESV)

God doesn't need me, but He wants me. God can command the sun, moon, and stars to worship, and they must obey. He is their Creator and is still all-powerful in every way. He created them for a purpose and for his glory. God can use the stars to change the life of a twenty-year-old, stubborn, rebellious young man. He can take someone who feels inadequate and gift him with a position in ministry. I don't pretend to know why God does the things He does. I quit trying to figure out all that God does a long time ago. I have just learned to trust in God's plan even when I don't understand the destination.

When I am struggling, I remember the stars. When I am questioning my value, I remember the stars. When I am questioning my calling, I remember the stars. I remember that God doesn't need me, but He wants me. He made everything we see, and I can't outrun him. My position, age, and relationship with God has changed over the years but the power of this truth still resonates in my heart. It isn't about my ability, talent, or wisdom. It is about the opportunity to serve and the Spirit of God who empowers us. God even tells us that he likes to use the weak.

1 Corinthians 1:26 — *"For consider your calling, brothers: not many of you were wise according to worldly standards, not many were powerful, not many were of noble birth."*

1 Corinthians 1:27 — *"But God chose what is foolish in the world to shame the wise; God chose what is weak in the world to shame the strong;"*

1 Corinthians 1:28 — *"God chose what is low and despised in the world, even things that are not, to bring to nothing things that are,"*

1 Corinthians 1:29 — *"so that no human being might boast in the presence of God."* (ESV)

I love this about God! He doesn't make the obvious choice. He doesn't only choose to use the star athlete, valedictorian, or beautiful people. He taps a guy like David on the shoulder and puts him in the game. He finds a guy like Moses hiding on the side of a mountain and sends him to change the world. He stops a man like Saul on his way to persecute Christians and says, "Let's go build a church." He looks for people like us and says, "You are exactly what I've been looking for." All of us have a chance to make a difference for the Kingdom of God. We love that God chooses to use the ordinary, but we still don't like to think of ourselves as ordinary. We idolize those who are extraordinary at the things the world values. Athletes, singers, musicians, or actors become our idols. Can I plead with you to be careful who you make your hero? Be careful who you try to emulate your life after. God isn't impressed by any of us. He doesn't need any of us...he already has the stars.

I have seven children now. My wife and I have six daughters and one son. His name is Gabe, in case you would like to remember him in your prayers. That is normally when people gasp and ask me, "Do you know where babies come from?" Yes, my wife and I know where kids come from. Some come from the hospital and others come from the foster system. Our children's ages span from sixteen to three. Three of our children are biologically our children. That means that God has blessed us with four children through adoption or custody. We have always wanted to help kids who were in need. Our years working with teenagers through our youth ministry gave us an understanding of what some kids face at home on a daily basis. When we answered the call of God on our life to be a foster family, we were praying for families to be restored. Adopting kids wasn't really part of our plan. Again, I have stopped trying to figure out what God is doing. I just trust him with the destination.

Adoption, and foster care, has touched the lives of all seven of our kids. Adding four children to our home changes things for our biological children as well. It also means that for four of our kids, their life story will always include a chapter of brokenness. I need my kids to understand the truth I learned gazing at the stars all those years ago. Our value isn't determined by our ability, background, or story. It is found in our calling and relationship with Jesus. If my kids allow their background to determine their value, they will always be left wondering if they are enough. I need them to know that they are enough. Not because of their story, but because of their Savior.

God can take the pieces of a rebellious young man and build a life beyond his most outrageous dreams. God can take their story of loss, brokenness, and adoption, and use it as a powerful picture of restoration. God may specialize in using the ordinary, but He creates things like the stars.

That is something so powerful about knowing Jesus. We may be ordinary people, but because of Jesus we don't have to spend our lives doing ordinary things. The lives of people committed to following Jesus do not blend in. Their lives shine in this world like those stars in the sky that night. At fourteen all I wanted to do was fit in. I wanted to blend in so that I could belong. That's the type of change that Jesus can make. Now my prayer is that I stand apart.

Your life can be brilliant, a shining example of all that God can do through an ordinary person. That is my deepest desire for myself, my wife, my children, and for you: that you would know the fullness of God's plan for your life. I hope that you come to experience the power of God's love and the freedom of finding your value in Him. It is a lesson that God is still teaching me.

Going from three children to seven brings a little bit of stress. Alright...that is a lie. It is crazy stressful and takes a ton of adjusting. I think that issues are magnified because we are trying to assimilate children into our home that are hurt and don't really want to be there. They just want their parents to get better so they can go home. My wife took the brunt of the stress as I was trying to lead a church through a global pandemic. I found myself reminding people that I missed the class in Bible college on "How to Shut Your Church Down." A good friend of mine described it this way. He said, "I thought we were running a marathon. When I got to the end, someone handed me a bike and informed me it was a triathlon."

Stress takes a toll on all of us in different ways. For my wife it came in the form of an autoimmune disease called alopecia. Alopecia causes hair to fall out in patches. In the most extreme cases those affected will lose all their hair. In one month, my wife went from having long, beautiful, red hair to shaving her head. To say it was emotional would be an understatement. Eventually my wife lost all her hair. I looked at her one day and said, "Who knew that I had a thing for bald women?" I find it helps to laugh through the tears. It would be easy to hide our insecurities, run from our weaknesses, or try to cover up the fact we have issues. My wife didn't do any of those things. She told people she was hurting, used the alopecia to build relationships with others, and has now helped multiple women through the process of finding wigs.

My wife has now started growing hair back. She currently has the sexiest short, snow white hair I have ever seen. I played an old Randy Travis song, "Forever and Ever, Amen," for her one day while we were riding in our car. The lyrics in the second verse go like this, "They say time takes its toll on a body. Makes the young girls' brown hair turn grey. But honey, I don't care, I ain't in love with your hair. And if it all fell out, well, I'd love you anyway." I am thankful for the alopecia because it has taught me to love my wife in a deeper way than I knew possible. I share this with you because my wife's value isn't found in her appearance. Her value is found in her calling and Savior. There are so many things we can't control in life. What we can control is how we use the things we experience.

Look at the stars! God values you more than them! You can come with the most broken background and a history full of mistakes. You can be the most ordinary among us. You might be unsure of your appearance and struggling with your value. Let your life shine for the glory of God! Let your life stand apart so that it can be used for the Kingdom. Embrace the truth that God doesn't need you, but He desperately wants you! We may be ordinary, but our God is extraordinary.

56

EPİLOGUE

CHAD P. SHEPHERD

The process of writing this book was a necessary time of intentional regeneration. Regeneration is such a pretty sounding word, but as anyone who has had physical rehabilitation knows, injured tissue sears with pain before the muscle becomes whole again.

Back in high school in the early 90s, I dated only one girl, the one that I married. As I've re-entered the dating scene as a second-time rookie, I've been frustrated when hearing potential dates say, "Well, I've been single for long enough now that I'm comfortable being alone." When I'd hear this, I'd think, "I don't want to be comfortable living alone; this solitary lifestyle is abysmal!" How ironic that statement sounded in my head as I realized that my loneliness was due to my own failure to rightly love my wife.

Only recently, during the writing of this book, I have been able to recognize that what I had before divorce was exactly what God had planned as his best path for me. There was no plan b. I had rejected the relationship that he had for me way back in my high school year of 1992. It has taken me two years of living in the desolation of divorce to face that reality. Even bigger than that, it has caused me to come face to face with a flaw within my own character. I can look back now and see my pattern of missing the blessings of the present while wishing for what I didn't have. Only in the presence of this loss have I been able to recognize the blessings that I'd so often missed. A full life stems from a grateful heart. Gratitude gives life.

Far too often I was fearful that I couldn't be enough, fearful that I'd lose what I had, and fearful that others saw me as somehow lesser than I was. Only now do I see that this was a one-two punch of my own selfish pride and believed lies from the enemy who still seeks to steal, kill, and destroy (Jn 10:10). So here I am, having suffered theft of mission, death of relationship, and destruction of my own life. Finally, in this place of desert, I find that the second half of that verse is a promise, every bit as potent as the warning in the first, "but I [Jesus] have come so that you might have life."

To the married who may be feeling the struggle of holding onto your family, all I can do is encourage you to reach out to God and find if there is any way for you to stay. If you're falling apart, agree to continue to reach closer to Him. This is especially true if you have children. I should have never abandoned the fight! All that Caleb, Aleks, and Sterling wanted from me was to remain their father, protect their home, and hold our family tightly no matter what pain this world could throw at them. I needed to look to find what was broken within myself so that I could continue to love my bride and be faithful to my vow. When their mother and I divorced, that foundation of home was shattered. This gave them a wound that will forever remain a visible scar. I was wrong. To my family, forgive me. I'm working to be a better man.

What I had was lost. Thank God, my kids are all still in my life. I give thanks for this! There is work yet to do, ground to be recovered, and love to be cultivated. I know now that part of the acceptance of my own failure is recognition that I must continue to walk on. I must be the best that I can be for them from this place forward, by the grace of God. These are lessons that I've learned late, but they are lessons that have great worth. God remains faithful.

Romans chapter five tells us that even while we were making choices that invited death and destruction (sin) into our lives, God still loved us and Jesus died for us. God, through his grace and wisdom, using even the acts of others, has made a way for me, purifying me day by day. Proverbs chapter sixteen talks about how pride leads to our own destruction, and I've found that to be true, but the truth does not end there. The restorative nature of God is greater than the destructive nature of the enemy of our souls. We see this reflected all around us. We see it in the rebirth in nature, new growth from fallen trees. We hear it in the laughter of our children and the stories of our grandparents. We feel it in the warmth of sunlight, and we see it every single morning with the rising of the sun. While death is present in this world, life wins again every single day. All that dies can be restored.

In the beginning, God spoke words that gave light to all existence and exploded the universe. He then began to form life and create the human soul and to exhale life into newly created lungs. Our first breath spoke his name, the exhale of his breath formed the first syllable, "Yah" and the inhale that followed whispered the second, "weh!" Even now, the very name of God is in our inhale and exhale, all of creation breathes his name, "Yahweh." His breath and light is here; it surrounds us with life. So take heart. As long as the sun still rises, as long as air still fills our lungs, our paths are not yet done. It is his nature to restore all things. Breathe deeply, give thanks for the blessings that you have, and walk on. We are all on this journey together, and perhaps we will cross paths along the way.

This is where I find myself. It is time to get up from the facedown dirt stance. I rise again, a man who perhaps is a little less arrogant, ready to "walk on" from my past self at this point. I'm still in the battle, but I do believe that God sees a victory. I still can't fathom what that looks like. My soul still mourns. Even so, I believe that it exists.

ABOUT THE AUTHORS

*C*had grew up in Preble County, Ohio with a bb-gun and his dog, Summers, running the creek-banks by day, and spending his nights in a treehouse by flashlight imagination. With a multi-generational lineage of steel-working, machining, Bible-banging, and moonshining, he grew up in the influence of the church, spiced with a splash of wild in his blood. Contentment was always elusive and caused him a constant search for meaning. His restless soul took him to Russia, China, destinations across Europe, and a four year stint in Guatemala. Along the way he pastored a church, principled a school, and ran relief work through the mountains of Central America. He has three times lost everything and four times started from scratch.

His three children are all smarter than he. Chad began writing in his blog, *Roaming the Countryside*, telling stories of his biological son, his two daughters, international adoption, and providing an unfiltered view of life as a missionary. The successes of his life are humbled by his loss of his marriage after 24 years. Chad is an ordained and licensed minister and has served as a drug task force chaplain with law enforcement. He studied psychology in his undergraduate work and has a Master of Arts in Christian Ministries from Anderson University. His tattoos tell the story of his life and his earrings reflect his tenacious spirit. He is a fan of epic tales and comeback stories. He holds out hope that his final chapters are not yet written.

Nancy grew up in Butler County, Ohio and lives in Middletown. She is the author of *I'm Still Here* and co-author of *Imagine You! 40 Day Devotional*. Nancy earned her B.S. in Secondary English and PreK-Elementary Education from BGSU and her M.Ed. and Ed.D from Miami University. She studied at Anderson University School of Theology and is a licensed and ordained minister in the Church of God. Co-founder of Grateful Heart Ministry with husband Darrell, Nancy enjoys her family and service to the community.